'A vital resource, this warm... beautifully written book will br... battle with conflicting and cripp... there has been a conspiracy of st... and depression in the Christ... powerfully helps to break that sil... reservation.'

Jeff Lucas, author, speaker, broadcaster

'This book is scientifically based and is very clear, accessible and positive in its message.'
Patricia Casey, author, journalist and Professor of Psychiatry at University College, Dublin

'Steve is a gift to the church as he has a unique ability to blend psychiatry with theology and academic insight with pastoral care. When writing on issues such as stress, depression and suicide, his style is informative, enlightening and extremely practical. If you are personally dealing with any of the topics covered or you are looking for greater knowledge and spiritual insight into mental health issues, this book is a must-read!'
Andrew McCourt, Teaching Pastor, Bayside Church, Roseville, California

'I wish I had read Dr Steve Critchlow's book 30 years ago. As a local church pastor, I have had to deal with people who have suffered with everything from anxiety to depression. I confess at times I was at a loss to know what to do. I had little or no understanding of what they were going through and most of the time could be of little help, except to support and comfort them in some way.

'This book gives a clear picture of what is really happening when people suffer from mental health problems and offers real insight into their conditions. However, the value of the book is not in its scholarly analysis but in the hope it brings to those who are suffering.

'There are no easy, get-well-quick solutions presented, but each chapter looks at common mental health problems and offers insight, help and advice. In particular, the insights into how we can help spiritually are refreshing, enlightening and powerful.

'My mother suffered from dementia, and I wish I had read this before her condition was diagnosed. It would have helped us immensely as a family.

'I would recommend that everyone read this book, especially those involved in pastoral work and counselling, and my friends in the medical profession.

'Steve's book, I believe, will be a modern classic and a major help to those of us dealing with people who suffer from depression and other related illnesses. Steve's book carries with it the weight of a professional psychiatrist and practitioner, but his easy-to-read and understandable style of writing makes it accessible to the public at large. I would have no hesitation in recommending it to those who suffer from mental illness – it will enable them to both better understand what is going on and find real help and hope.'

Paul Reid, Pastor Emeritus, Christian Fellowship Church, Strandtown, Belfast

'Dr Critchlow has spoken on many occasions to groupings at Clonard Monastery, Belfast. Those attending found his talks most interesting, easy to follow and practical to implement. His combination of modern psychiatric study with a living spirituality was unique and inspiring. He has a wealth of knowledge and experience and shares it in an appropriate way with people. Making his teaching available in written form can only be a great benefit to those who may be seeking help and understanding.'

Fr Michael Murtagh, Former Rector, Clonard Monastery, Belfast

'I am delighted that Dr Critchlow has put into book format the content of these talks which he has been doing all around the country for some years now. As a Christian counsellor and church leader, I have been very concerned to help people both in the church and in the wider community, who are struggling with the issues of depression, anxiety and suicidal thoughts. I have invited Steve to give his talks in the towns in our region and have found them to be very well received and a great help to people in understanding, both from a medical and spiritual point of view, their feelings and how to handle them better. I warmly commend these talks. I just wish that my pastoral training had included his material.

'In his treatment of these issues, Dr Critchlow comes across with a lovely "bedside manner" which gives you the sense that he really understands and empathises. At the same time he brings a clear analysis of the condition and very practical guidelines as to how one can be helped. This book will be a real handbook for the pastoral carer, counsellor or friend who wants to understand how to help and support someone suffering with some of these very debilitating conditions. I especially appreciate the combination of the psychiatric expertise of an experienced professional together with the spiritual wisdom of the Scriptures. I have welcomed a move away from the old Freudian treatment of religion as a neurosis to a more holistic appreciation of the value of faith and spiritual experience in our overall well-being. Well done, Steve! May your book be widely used to bring practical wisdom and help to those struggling in these areas!'
Graeme Wylie BSc, MTh, DipCouns, MIACC; Director, Hope Counselling; Former Leader of Plumbline Ministries, Ireland

'This is a subject of which local churches know little. Often the stigma attached to mental illness means that many people will simply not feel that they can talk freely about how they feel. Providing wise, considered and yet clear spiritual leadership for both individuals and the church family in this subject is a huge challenge. Steve ably helps us as church leaders to bridge this gap. He uses his wealth of professional expertise along with his own experience of leading spiritually, to carve out for us a clear pathway for understanding mental illness as well as demonstrating how biblical faith can revolutionise lives that are blighted by such illness. I wholeheartedly commend his well thought-out instruction.'

Adrian Lowe, Pastor, Amblecote Community Church

Mindful of the Light

Practical help and spiritual hope for mental health

Stephen Critchlow

instant apostle

First published in Great Britain in 2016

Instant Apostle
The Barn
1 Watford House Lane
Watford
Herts
WD17 1BJ

British Library Cataloguing-in-Publication Data

A catalogue record for this book is available from the British Library

This book and all other Instant Apostle books are available from Instant Apostle:

Website: www.instantapostle.com

E-mail: info@instantapostle.com

ISBN 978-1-909728-44-8

Printed in Great Britain

Instant Apostle is a way of getting ideas flowing, between followers of Jesus, and between those who would like to know more about His Kingdom.

It's not just about books and it's not about a one-way information flow. It's about building a community where ideas are exchanged. Ideas will be expressed at an appropriate length. Some will take the form of books. But in many cases ideas can be expressed more briefly than in a book. Short books, or pamphlets, will be an important part of what we provide. As with pamphlets of old, these are likely to be opinionated, and produced quickly so that the community can discuss them.

Well-known authors are welcome, but we also welcome new writers. We are looking for prophetic voices, authentic and original ideas, produced at any length; quick and relevant, insightful and opinionated. And as the name implies, these will be released very quickly, either as Kindle books or printed texts or both.

Join the community. Get reading, get writing and get discussing!

instant apostle

Disclaimer

None of the material in this book should be seen as giving definitive advice on individual mental health issues. This is the province of locally based professionals.

Names in the book have been changed to preserve anonymity.

Dedication

I dedicate the book to my dear wife, Rosalind, to whom I have been very happily married for the last 36 years. She says life has never been boring being married to me! Not only as a wife, but also as a wonderful friend and mother of our five daughters, she has been through all the vicissitudes of life with me. I cannot thank her enough.

Acknowledgements

I wish to thank the following for reading the initial drafts of the book and making encouraging and detailed comments, which were extremely helpful.

Chris Elston is a good friend and English teacher, with whom I have stayed several times on recent trips to Moldova. His comments on my use of English were instructive. Dr Jim Ferguson, Jim Thompson and I meet together to share our hearts and lives every few months in Belfast. Their comments on the structure of the book were very helpful. Professor Arthur Williamson is my brother-in-law and has been a lecturer in social administration but also involved professionally in mental health in Northern Ireland. I valued his comments on sections of the material. Recently a few Christian psychiatrists have been meeting together in Belfast and Dr Ken Yeow has been part of this group. He made important contributions on points of psychiatric information. Marijke Hoek added several valuable points as she read the book on behalf of Instant Apostle. I was delighted that Professor Patricia Casey was able to read the manuscript and offer several helpful suggestions prior to publication.

Finally, my dear wife, Rosalind, has made numerous contributions, the usual one being, 'You can't say that!' and has read several drafts, helping with structure and finer points.

Many, many thanks to you all.

Contents

General introduction

Over the last four years, I have been giving courses of talks for the general public on mental health topics. I have been very encouraged by the many people who have attended and the way in which they have responded to these talks. I have been surprised by the courage of those with mental health issues who have openly talked about their bipolar illness and their struggles with alcohol and depression. Some have shared about the terrible loss they have experienced, following a death in the family from suicide. They have found it so difficult to move on in their lives following this event. Someone came to a talk recently, deeply affected by a young man he knew who had died by suicide, and now he wanted to learn how to help in suicide prevention. Many have come to be informed. Others have attended wanting to find support and help, as they have felt fragile and exhausted with the burden of caring for someone who is mentally ill. Mental health professionals have attended, and it has been interesting and helpful at times to have their expertise. Often we have invited local mental health charities, and their contributions have been very valuable.

There have been two main aims behind these talks:

- First of all, I wanted to give accurate information on important mental health issues, so the first challenge has been to adapt knowledge and information on these topics for the needs of very varied audiences. This is not a textbook on mental health, but a presentation of some very real problems that many people face.

- Secondly, I wanted to show how the Christian faith relates to mental health. These days, the Christian faith tends to be sidelined in the public arena. Faith is perceived to be a purely personal issue. Raising faith issues in the workplace is often frowned upon. However, the question sensitively put, 'Do you have a faith that helps you in these stormy and difficult times that you are going through?' is often appropriate. To find out about the beliefs and spiritual support structures of an individual is an important part of a full psychiatric assessment, and this is often neglected. It is reasonable when someone expresses religious belief to consider asking the person whether he or she has considered the possibility of seeking help from an appropriate spiritual leader or counsellor.

The Christian faith was never intended to be a private affair. Jesus talks about His kingdom coming, and in the Lord's Prayer we are taught to pray, 'your kingdom come, your will be done, on earth as it is in heaven' (Matthew 6:10).

This kingdom is not meant to be silent and hidden. Rather, those who follow the King are encouraged to be like lights shining in the darkness so all can see the light.

That is why, in these talks, the spiritual dimension has been included.

However, my intention has always been to be sensitive to the many and varied audiences who have attended. For this reason the talks have been in two parts with an intermission in between. The spiritual aspects of the topic have been discussed in the second part, so that those who do not wish to stay for these need not. Likewise, in this book, spiritual topics are dealt with in separate chapters.

Increasingly, people have been requesting copies of my notes following the talks, and whilst I have been happy to provide these, I have now decided to make them available in book form. I did not want to present the teaching as one might do in a formal talk, so some of the material has been adapted to show the journey of the patient through the various conditions mentioned.

In the book, I use a number of case histories. These are mainly fictitious and are not intended to refer to any specific individuals. In some places I have described events from my own experience, and I have also used some other true life stories.

Now just a little about myself. I have spent many years as a consultant psychiatrist working for the National Health Service in the United Kingdom and am based in Northern Ireland. I began life in Stockport, Cheshire, and attended Stockport Grammar School. I did my medical training at Fitzwilliam College, Cambridge and then King's College Hospital, London. When Ros and I married in 1979, we spent our first four years together in Galway in the west of Ireland, thoroughly enjoying the Irish way of life and our contact with many students from University

College, Galway. Then it was back to London where I began psychiatric training in St Bartholomew's Hospital, London. My registrar was Dr Ted Dinan, and Professor Anthony Clare (of BBC Radio 4 Extra's programme *In the Psychiatrist's Chair*) taught us interviewing skills.

During this time I led different churches in the London area as part of the Ichthus Christian Fellowship in Forest Hill. The excellent teaching of Roger Forster and others, and the preachers' workshops I attended, were very important in helping me grow in leadership. At a Eurofire conference in Birmingham, God met me in a new way with the result that in early 1990 my wife and I, with our five daughters and 37 pieces of hand luggage, left the UK to spend the next six and a half years in Cyprus.

Initially we were based in Limassol, and then Nicosia. We have many Cypriot friends from this time. In Nicosia we began spending much time with people from Sri Lanka and were delighted to see some churches start amongst them. Although I cannot visit these churches in Cyprus (and now also in Israel) as often as I would wish, with the benefits of modern technology such as Skype, I can still do a weekly Bible lesson for many of them. For the first two and a half years in Cyprus I was not in medical practice, but then over the next four years returned to the UK for short-term locum positions, mainly in General Adult Psychiatry.

We then came to Belfast for the next ten years and were so appreciative of the way Dr Mulryne and Methodist College received our five daughters. For me it was back to full-time psychiatry, and I began to specialise in psychiatry of the elderly, taking up a consultant position in Holywell

Hospital, Antrim between 1999 and 2006. We joined a local church in Cregagh, East Belfast, where I served as an elder for several years.

In 2006, we moved to Birmingham for three years where I took a position as Director of Lifehope, a ministry of Operation Mobilisation, founded by George Verwer, who has been a great support and encouragement to us over the years. Then we enjoyed living in Prato, near Florence, Italy, for a year. We learned Italian, worked on 24/7 prayer with several Italian churches in the area, and spent much of our time with people from mainland China who made up a third of the population of the city.

On returning to Belfast, I celebrated my sixtieth birthday by returning to psychiatry, this time as a locum consultant in the psychiatry of the elderly, before taking a second retirement from clinical practice in January 2015. Life has been very varied!

From this fairly broad background, I have been able to examine mental health issues from both psychiatric and spiritual perspectives. I believe this is helpful, and I trust you will agree.

I hope you will find the material useful.

Stephen Critchlow, summer 2015

Introduction to mental health issues

Sigmund Freud, the influential Austrian psychoanalyst, believed that religious belief was a sign of weakness and indicative of 'neurosis'. He claimed that the idea of God was not a lie, but a device of the unconscious. With comments like these it is easy to see why many psychiatrists have viewed religious belief with puzzlement, disinterest or, indeed, frank disdain. In the past, surveys have shown that patients have had stronger belief in God than did their psychiatrists. At times psychiatrists have been guilty of negative and unhelpful advice to patients regarding their religious beliefs. No doubt this has been influenced at times by the colourful nature of religious delusions, when some patients have been in a very disturbed state.

On the other hand, some religious leaders have not helped matters. Mental illness has often been seen as the person's own fault. The impression has been given that it must be the result of spiritual problems or lack of commitment. The sufferer has been loaded with guilt on top of their psychiatric problems. Often the person might sense failure or inadequacy on having been told to 'pull yourself together', without being shown the mercy and compassion which they needed and deserved. At times psychiatry and religion have seemed poles apart. Thankfully, this situation is changing. Many church leaders have been actively seeking training so they can better understand mental illness. In the psychiatric profession there has been a considerable shift in opinion over the last 15 years or so. The Royal College of Psychiatrists has a special interest group set up to look at spiritual issues, and there have been many papers appearing in prestigious journals, examining the link between psychiatry and religious beliefs. One of these papers is entitled 'The psychosocial benefits of religious practice', written by Professor Patricia Casey. It will be referred to several times in this book.

Men and women are spiritual as well as emotional beings. However, the spiritual aspect has often been ignored by mental health professionals. Indeed, an understanding of the significance of religious belief and spiritual matters in mental health is largely missing or simply glossed over in most psychiatric textbooks.

Another difficulty faced in psychiatry and by patients with mental illness is the problem of stigma. Stigma fuels negative opinions about people with mental illness. Such negative thoughts about those who are mentally ill may cloud our judgement. They may also affect our relationships with those who struggle with mental illness. Those who suffer may be perceived as being dangerous, unpredictable, and having only themselves to blame. They may be regarded as being unwilling to help themselves, or may be seen as people who will never improve or recover completely. They may be considered as being very different from ourselves. Stigma tends to exclude people and push them away. It becomes a way of putting people in a box and then quietly ignoring them, or even castigating them.

After a five-year research programme The Royal College of Psychiatrists found that there was some evidence that stigma could be reduced.[1]

Around one in four people will need treatment of some kind for a mental health condition at some time in their lives. Since many others will be involved as carers in various capacities, it would be reasonable to suggest that almost all of us will be affected by mental health issues. I am hopeful that the mental health topics covered here will provide information and hope to those who suffer from mental health problems and their many dedicated carers. I also believe the material will be of great benefit to Christian leaders and those with whom they have contact, who may struggle with mental health issues.

---

[1] A. Crisp, M. Gelder, E. Goddard and H. Meltzer. 'Stigmatization of people with mental illnesses: a follow-up study within the Changing Minds campaign of The Royal College of Psychiatrists.' *World Psychiatry*, 4:2, 106-113 '(June 2005).

Chapter one
The person with stress and anxiety

How does the body respond to stress?

Stress is a feature of everyday life. It is difficult to conceive of a life without stress. There are pressures upon us of things that must be done today and urgent deadlines that must be met. There are stresses in difficult relationships, financial and employment concerns, time pressures... the list seems endless!

Pressure can sometimes be helpful to us. Life without stress could be very boring. When we are under stress, the body is threatened and reacts accordingly. We call this the 'fight or flight reaction'. Imagine that you are in a field with an angry bull. The best response, no doubt, is to run faster than ever before, and jump higher than ever before over the fence to reach safety. However, if one was a fledgling matador, armed with a sword, one might choose to stay and fight the bull.

This fight or flight reaction is something that is inbuilt in humankind. It is a safety device. What happens in the body is that there is a massive outpouring of a substance

24

called adrenaline that prepares us for action. It causes the muscles to tense and helps us to be ready for either fight or flight. The difficulty, however, is that if increased adrenaline production is maintained over a long period of time, then it can result in mental or physical exhaustion.

How can we understand stress and the difficulties in coping with it?

Often this can be understood as a mismatch between external demands and the ability to cope. A certain amount of stress is good for us, but if the stress becomes too much, then there is a mismatch between the stress and our ability to deal with it.

What is the connection between stress and performance?

There is a famous diagram called the Yerkes–Dodson curve (see following page). [1] This relates the quality of performance to the level of arousal. For example, when the level of arousal is very low, one is not expecting quality performance. This might be, for example, when we are asleep. A little higher arousal, and then we might be awake, feeling bored, but really not doing very much. There is a certain minimal quality of performance and a relatively low level of arousal. On the other hand, on the way to work, on the bus or train, we might feel mildly alert as we are pondering the problems of the day ahead and how we are going to deal with them. The quality of our performance is rising, and the level of our arousal is also rising. And then at the top of the curve is the optimal level where we are performing well and the level of arousal is moderately high. This might be the state we would like to imagine we are in all the time, when we are working, or when we are doing something that is demanding of our time and attention.

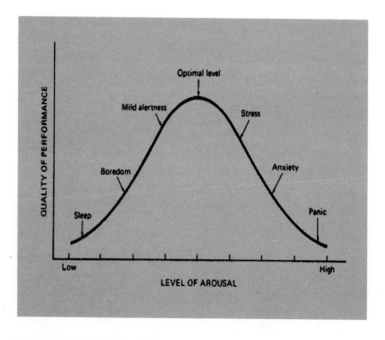

However, beyond the top of the curve the level of arousal is continuing to rise, and now what happens is the quality of performance tends to decline. We are aware of feeling stressed. This might be the situation when we are under time pressure. We feel we have to do a number of things in a certain amount of time, and we begin to feel the stress levels rise. Further down the curve one feels anxious. The level of arousal is now very high, and we are not able to manage easily the demands placed upon us. Our performance levels have declined. When the level of arousal is very high, performance levels fall off considerably and we may be in a state of panic.

Here is Ruth's story.

Her mother bottle-fed her as an infant and had a lot of her own problems. As a single parent she had to keep working to try and support her three children, of whom Ruth was the youngest. Ruth, even from an early age, was left with childminders and there were several of these, with little consistency in care. When her mother came home from work, she was exhausted from her long day of cleaning offices, and Ruth tended to be left in her cot for many hours by herself. Ruth remembers her mother being anxious about everything, and it seemed, as she grew up, that Ruth absorbed her mother's anxiety. Some days she was left in the care of her uncle, an older man, and one day he did something to Ruth that even now she finds difficult to discuss, and she never told her mother.

She found the first days at school very difficult. She felt so alone and was badly teased by the other children. She was afraid of the dark and needed the light to be left on at night. She found tests at school very difficult. She would lie awake for hours at night worrying about the test she had to do the following day. She wet her bed till the age of seven and bit her nails right back. As a teenager she remembers worrying about everything. There was a time when she was 15 that she clearly remembers. She had to visit the dentist, but on the way there, she became so anxious that she passed out on the stairs leading to the dentist's surgery. Then this happened again a few months later in the local supermarket. She remembers that she felt very short of breath and then felt a big wave of panic surge over her. She thought she was going to die as she felt so awful. She had an uncomfortable sensation of feeling very unreal, and then she must have passed out, for the next thing she remembers was the sales assistant gently supporting her and asking if she was all right. She felt

27

terribly embarrassed and even now, several years later, feels she cannot go back to that same store. She feels too ashamed and worries that the same thing could happen again.

Her panic attacks have tended to recur. Sometimes she can manage for a week without getting one, but they often occur two to three times a week. One happened at her place of employment, and she has now been off work for six months and is unsure if she will manage to go back. She still lives at home with her mother, but does not go out much these days because she feels afraid she might have further panic attacks.

She still lies awake most nights for a couple of hours before she can get off to sleep. She feels exhausted a lot of the time, and frequently gets headaches. Sometimes she feels short of breath, even at home, and often gets pins and needles in her hands and feet. When she gets very anxious, she tends to spend a lot of time on her own in her room. She has been given Valium (a minor tranquilliser that can be addictive) by her doctor to try to ease the anxiety, but frequently finishes the week's supply of tablets after three or four days, and her doctor has said she will not give her any more. She has begun to keep a few tins of lager by her bed in case she feels very bad.

A few weeks ago she was out and felt terrible. This time she also developed a bad pain in her chest. 'I thought I was having a heart attack,' she said. Her mother, who was with her, rushed her to the local Accident and Emergency department. They did a range of tests, but said that everything was normal. They explained that with a panic attack, a person can get severe chest pain. It was just that she had never had this kind of pain before, and she had been very worried about it.

She is worried about the future, because unless things change and she can find help, she is concerned that she might not get back to work, and at present her social life is almost non-existent. She has been drinking and is wondering how she can manage without the alcohol to help calm her nerves.

What is anxiety?

Anxiety is the feeling of fear that we get when faced with threatening or difficult situations. We may suddenly be faced with a demand that is placed upon us, which we feel unable to deal with. A threatening situation may arise, and we are not quite sure how to respond. People may struggle when facing difficult problems. They may try to seek to allay the anxiety. There are different ways of doing this, and anxiety is linked to heavy alcohol use, smoking and addiction problems. As well as this, sleep disorders and depression may ensue. Anxiety tends to be lower in married people. It tends to be higher in those who are single, separated or divorced. Anxiety is twice as common in women as it is in men.[2]

What are the causes of anxiety?

In childhood, the first three years are very important. This is the time during which the child bonds closely with its mother. Occasionally, this bonding can be with a mother substitute. During this period of bonding, the child learns that its needs will be met, and there will be a response of love, with fulfilment of its requirements from its mother. If this procedure is disturbed, and the child gets 'double messages', sometimes being loved and nurtured and on other occasions experiencing rejection, then there are difficulties in the bonding process, and these can be reflected in later life.

In Ruth's case, her mother was often away, and she was left with a variety of childminders. Even when her mother was there, she was often too exhausted to pay attention to Ruth's needs. If the child experiences physical or sexual abuse or neglect, then again the child may suffer as a result. Ruth was abused by her uncle. She still carries this experience with her and has vivid dreams in which she relives it, and wakes up screaming and in a cold sweat. She has still not been able to tell her mother about it.

If there is demand for excessive conformity and overemphasis on achievements, then this again may cause anxiety in the child, who may then develop an anxious personality. When I asked patients who suffered from anxiety how long they had been anxious, the answer was often as long as they could remember. Certainly, this was true for Ruth. She was very anxious even as a young child. Anxiety does seem to be more common in some families than others. Exactly to what extent this link is genetic and to what extent it is conditioned by early environment is difficult to establish fully. Ruth's mother was very anxious, and her brother also tends to be anxious.

How may long-term problems and life events affect us?

People can be vulnerable to anxiety because of ongoing poor relationships. Single mothers who bring up children on their own often report anxiety. Poor housing, poverty and unemployment are other issues that may be long-term and may lead to anxiety.

Various life events often cause us to be anxious. These can be events happening at work or school. Ruth faced a lot of problems at school with being teased and finding school tests very difficult. Serious illness can be a cause of anxiety. Many people suffer anxiety about their personal appearance or sexual development. Others may have existential anxiety about the meaning of life and similar issues. Certain medications cause anxiety as a side effect. Illicit drugs such as amphetamines and cocaine can cause marked anxiety, as can withdrawal from prohibited drugs such as heroin or prescribed drugs such as Valium.

How may fear and anxiety affect us? There are three areas which I wish to consider.

- The first is how fear and anxiety can affect our minds.

- Secondly, how feeling anxious can affect our bodies.

- Thirdly, how it can affect relationships.

1. How can fear and anxiety affect our minds?

We may be hyper-alert or apprehensive. We may feel 'on edge'. We are aware of feeling anxious and worried. We may feel that we are unable to face particular situations. We may have particular phobias and fears of certain situations. It could be, for example, a fear of flying, or a fear of spiders, or a fear of close spaces. Phobias are quite common. Agoraphobia is the fear of being in an open space (traditionally the marketplace), now more commonly understood as a fear of going out. Sometimes people with phobias can live closed lives, remaining, even for years, in the same situation because they find that they cannot face the difficulty of going into the outside world. Ruth was often very anxious and worried. She is now going out less because of her anxieties and fears.

Those with anxiety may suffer from poor concentration. People may complain of poor memory. When they do so, it is important to check that the memory is actually intact. I had several people coming to a memory clinic complaining of poor memory, and on testing there was no significant deficit. However, when I enquired about their difficulties, I found that they often had stressful jobs and had problems in concentrating. When concentration is a problem, information is not absorbed correctly, and the person thinks that he or she has a poor memory.

People may feel exhausted and depressed as a result of anxiety. They may be tearful. In this case, careful assessment is always important to clarify that the situation is a problem of anxiety, and not anxiety and depression mixed together. Particularly in the elderly, anxiety can be a harbinger of depression, and it is important to have ruled out depression before treating the anxiety. The person may be irritable or quick to anger. Sometimes a situation can occur where the person feels unreal. Ruth found these feelings of unreality very difficult to cope with. Sometimes the person may feel that the situation around them has changed. These feelings of unreality are called depersonalisation (where one feels unreal in oneself) and derealisation (when it seems the environment is unreal).

2. How may anxiety affect our bodies?

Most people recognise tension headaches resulting from stress and anxiety. They will also recognise the feeling of a dry mouth when facing a difficult situation, such as a job interview. Sleep disturbances are common. Often there is a difficulty in getting off to sleep because of anxious thoughts. Breathing may be affected as those with anxiety tend to feel short of breath, and as a result may breathe more rapidly.

Ruth had periods when she felt very short of breath. In these situations she tended to increase the rate of her breathing and noticed that this tended to make her feel dizzy. She also had frequent headaches and difficulty sleeping.

There is frequently an increased sensitivity to noise. Many may recognise palpitations, or increased awareness of the heartbeat, and indeed the heart rate may be faster when a person is anxious. People will often feel tiredness or weariness in their bones and muscles. I used to find, in my outpatient clinic, individuals commonly complained of feeling fatigued and weary all the time. This was the case with Ruth. She felt continually exhausted, and although she had seen her doctor about this, he had told her that there was nothing physically the matter. Although there can be different causes of fatigue and exhaustion, it can be a result of persistent anxiety. People may also feel tightness or pain in the chest or jaw. Again, it is important to consider other possible causes before attributing these to anxiety. People may find that they feel a lump in their throat or a sense of their stomach churning. Others complain of irritable bowel and irregular bowel movements. Feelings of giddiness or unsteadiness may be present. Actual faints may occur.

There may be increased perspiration, and the hands may feel cold and clammy. Pins and needles may be felt in the arms and legs. Nausea and diarrhoea can occur, and there can sometimes be difficulty in swallowing with severe anxiety. Increased frequency of passing urine is often noticed, and others complain of ringing in the ears.

3. What are some of the interpersonal effects of anxiety?

People with anxiety tend to react in one of two ways. On the one hand, when people are feeling very anxious, they can tend to withdraw from family and friends and general social activities. This is often to avoid the anxiety-provoking situation or to allow themselves space to work through their anxious feelings. This was what happened to Ruth. She began to spend a lot of time in her room. She kept trying to work through her difficulties, but found her thoughts just went round and round in her head, and she felt she was getting nowhere.

On the other hand, some people react with irritability towards others. There can be angry outbursts or lashing out and even physical violence as a result of the anxiety.

How can we understand panic attacks?

Many people do not realise the effects of overbreathing. I have mentioned above that people may breathe more frequently in anxiety, because they feel short of breath. However, what tends to happen in this situation is as follows. The overbreathing sets up a vicious cycle. The carbon dioxide in the blood is exhaled through the lungs and the level of carbon dioxide in the blood falls. This fall continues as the person carries on breathing rapidly. The level of oxygen remains relatively constant. However, this falling carbon dioxide level causes small arteries, called arterioles, in the brain to begin to constrict. This reduces the circulation of blood to the brain, and the person experiences a sense of faintness or dizziness. The person may breathe even more rapidly because of these uncomfortable feelings. If this continues long enough, then the person might faint.

In panic attacks there is shortness of breath. There are often feelings of smothering and choking. Palpitations are common. In around 40 per cent there may be chest pain or discomfort. This shortness of breath and chest pain had caused Ruth and her mother to look for help in the Accident and Emergency department, because Ruth thought she was having a heart attack.

An individual will often be perspiring heavily. There may be feelings of unreality – a person might feel unreal, or the area around the person may seem unreal. There is often numbness and tingling. There may be trembling or shaking episodes. There may be a fear of losing one's mind and going crazy. In a panic attack the individual often feels completely out of control. The person may feel that they are going to do something terrible, or there may even be a fear of dying. These feelings can be extremely unpleasant.

When Ruth fainted in the supermarket she said to herself that she would never return. This fear of being out of control may cause the person to restrict their activities. There is a connection between panic attacks and agoraphobia (fear of going out). Ruth began to show signs of this, and started to reduce her activities. She began to be afraid of going out alone, and now preferred to go out with her mother.

How can we manage stress?

Stress is often related to anxiety, and learning to identify the sources of stress in our lives can be very important. A stress diary can be very helpful. If a person can be encouraged to write down their perceived stresses in a daily diary, then this may help clarify the sources of the stress. Some causes are more obvious than others. For example, problems with time management and trying to do too much can be issues. There can be pressures from relationships with other people. Sometimes the sources of stress are internal problems in our lives that are unresolved. Stress can result from difficult habits against which the person battles. When the sources of stress are identified, these can guide us towards making necessary adjustments. The difficulty with anxiety and stress is that problems tend to revolve in our minds as we ruminate on them. This was a problem for Ruth, when she went to her room. Her anxious thoughts kept going round in her head, and she could make no progress in resolving them.

When considering stress, we often find it very easy to blame others for it. Also, we can find it easy to blame circumstances and the general pressures of life. However, if we are going to deal with stress effectively, it is important that we take responsibility for the stress in our lives as far as possible.

Are there unhelpful ways of coping with stress?

People will sometimes smoke heavily, drink heavily, or overeat. Others might use drugs or alcohol to help them relax. This, however, can lead to drug and alcohol dependence. Ruth had become concerned about her drinking. She was using a lot of Valium and had begun to drink to try to deal with her anxiety levels. This was placing her at considerable risk of dependence.

A person might collapse for hours in front of the television or computer, but this usually does not help to resolve the underlying anxiety. Many people procrastinate rather than face the problems, but this rarely helps. Others try to fill up every minute of the day to avoid looking at difficult issues in their lives. Still others may withdraw from people or activities. Again, some might interact negatively with other people who may be perceived as causing the stress. All of these tend to be unhelpful ways of dealing with the problem. Often, when stressed, we may drink more tea and coffee or even cola than normal. However, one needs to understand the high caffeine content of many of these drinks. I can clearly remember, as a junior doctor, being on duty every other night and sometimes being extremely tired. I tried to counter this by drinking a lot of coffee, but I became aware of being on edge in a way that was not normal for me. Excess caffeine can be detrimental to people with a tendency towards anxiety.

How should we deal with stress?

* The first way we may deal with stress is by avoiding it. Sometimes we need to learn to say 'no' to requests from other people. This is not easy for those of us who prefer to try to please whenever possible – I tend to be like this. However, there are situations in my life when I have learned to say 'no' to demands placed upon me. For example, I was recently asked to write a series of articles for a newspaper, but realised that this would take a lot of time, and it was not a priority, so I declined. Learning to say 'no' to the demands of others may be necessary. We need, however, to be careful and wise in what we choose to avoid.

* Secondly, we can deal with stress by changing our behaviour. For example, stress may result from difficult relationships with others. We may find that we have responded to a certain person in the same way for a long time, despite recognising that this causes us pressure and anxiety. We may find it difficult to confront this situation. For example, somebody else may be making demands on us, and we go along with their suggestions. This, however, becomes an ongoing source of strain and anxiety for us. It may become necessary to face up to this and ask to talk to the person, in a planned way, about the situation, and how their attitudes and actions may be causing us stress. Again, we need to be careful how we do this, and preferably go into this kind of situation calmly, so that the situation does not get out of hand. Learning to deal with the pressures resulting

from difficult relationships can be very important in our lives.

- The third way of dealing with stress is to learn to adapt. For example, there are people who are perfectionists. If they believe that all the time they have to achieve perfection in every activity they set their hands to, then life will be quite difficult for them. The perfectionist may need to adapt whilst still maintaining appropriate standards.

- Fourthly, there is the reality that what doesn't kill us often makes us stronger. Sometimes we need to learn to accept a degree of stress. For example, when learning to drive we might well feel stressed. However, we recognise that the result of passing the driving test is worthwhile. And that means that we will accept the necessary degree of stress in order to pass the test. (However, on the other hand, as a father with five daughters, having taught some of them to drive, I think that this stress is probably best avoided!)

- Another situation we may need to accept is that although we might talk to a person about the stress we experience in our relationship with them, we cannot control the other person's response, and they might continue to treat us in an unhelpful way. Sometimes it can be useful to involve a friend or mediator in this situation. We can learn, if necessary, to forgive the person and then find alternative approaches to deal with the ongoing difficulties.

In what ways can we deal with anxiety?

Many people need to discover simple ways to relax. These, of course, can be varied, depending on the individual. Personally, I find walking and exercise valuable. Strengthening our physical health increases our ability to deal with stress. The reason why physical exercise is very beneficial, in both prevention and treatment of depression and anxiety, may be related to the release of substances called endorphins in the brain, which tend to reduce anxiety and bring on a sense of relaxation. Group-based physical exercise is particularly beneficial.

Ensuring that we get enough sleep can be very important. Simple techniques of sleep hygiene, as it is called, can be beneficial. What is sleep hygiene? This involves not sleeping during the day, but sleeping properly at night. It involves avoiding excess caffeine particularly in the afternoons and evenings. A gentle walk in the early evening can induce a sense of restfulness. Sometimes people find a milky drink is very helpful before retiring to bed. It is helpful to establish regular sleeping and waking patterns – aiming to go to bed and wake up at approximately the same time each day. Learning to deal with anxious thoughts earlier in the day and at least before retiring to bed is important. However, if one is in bed in a very restless and wakeful state, it is probably better to get out of bed and face the difficulties before trying to go to sleep again. Writing down anxious thoughts and, next to them, possible solutions can be very valuable. Sometimes nothing can be done about certain anxiety-provoking situations, and realising this can help us turn away from the anxious thoughts connected with them. Often, however, something can be done and, if so, it is better to do it, or make a reminder note about doing it the next day. Some people, including myself, find it helpful to have paper and pen by the bedside, so if an anxious thought comes along I can write it down and remember to deal with it the following morning.

What other ways can we use to relax?

Giving time to friends and ensuring good relationships is extremely important. Some people find enjoying music or gardening or taking a hot bath or massage are very relaxing. Pets can help calm people who are anxious. Learning to appreciate nature, or books, or comedy programmes can be helpful. Scheduling a definite relaxation time each day can be very important. When I have been extremely busy I have found it helpful to plan one hour a day when I do something purely relaxing. Keeping a sense of humour is important. We should learn to avoid self-medication with alcohol, drugs and cigarettes, and reducing our caffeine intake may be necessary.

How can time management help?

Almost without exception, stressed patients find it difficult to estimate how long a task will take. For example, on the way to the shops, unexpected events such as a phone call or difficulties with parking may occur, and then the estimated time given for the task will be very much exceeded. Learning to accept that interruptions will happen, and learning to plan accordingly is a vital ability.

People struggling to manage their time need to learn the following skill. Often they will think of the many things which they believe must be squeezed into a certain time span. They may start on the list and try valiantly to squeeze all the activities into this time interval. However, this is likely to lead to stress, which then reduces efficiency and is likely to be counterproductive. It is much better to say to oneself, 'I have a certain amount of time. What jobs can be done effectively in this time?' If things cannot be done through lack of time, then they should be postponed to another time, or delegated, or simply left. Learning to manage time this way can be helpful.

In what other ways can we learn to deal with anxiety and stress?

One of the simple methods is to learn breathing techniques. These are relatively easy to learn, but the difficulty is that people tend to forget to practise them when they are feeling anxious or stressed. These techniques might be of particular value to someone like Ruth, as mentioned above, if she could learn them and then practise them when faced with severe stress. She could then feel back in control of her life, rather than being dominated by her anxiety and panic attacks.

The technique of controlled breathing is to slow down the breathing, as follows. The person is instructed to breathe in to a slow count of four, and to breathe out to a count of seven. One should breathe in through the nose and out through the mouth, using the abdomen as much as possible and the chest wall as little as possible. Learning to breathe slowly and deeply like this induces a sense of relaxation and calm. In a situation that might induce panic, just to sit down and do this can be helpful. Practising breathing techniques such as these can bring back a sense of being in control again.

Progressive muscular relaxation is another method that is helpful. In this technique, the person, to the count of six, gradually tenses a muscle group and then holds the tension to the count of six, and then releases the tension again to the count of six. The muscle groups are in turn stretched and relaxed group by group. Usually a start is made with the feet, then the calves, followed by the thighs, then the abdomen and chest, then the arms and hands, followed by the neck and finally the shoulders and face. Muscular relaxation with breathing techniques combines the benefits of both.

Other techniques of relaxation involve use of the imagination. For example, one might imagine oneself on a beach or near a lake in a very restful position. Calm background music often helps. There are relaxation tapes that one can play to assist in this process. In the many types of relaxation treatment available it can be important to ask the question, 'What is the underlying basis of this treatment?'

Many treatments are fine and helpful, whereas some, such as yoga, have their roots in Hindu beliefs.

What is Mindfulness?

Over recent years, many people have been using 'Mindfulness' strategies to help them cope with stress and anxiety. Mindfulness, although a term in English usage since the sixteenth century, has been particularly associated with Buddhist religious practice. Jon Kabat-Zinn, a major proponent, describes five core principles of mindfulness meditation:[3]

- There is increasing awareness of internal and external experience. The external ones are experienced through the five senses, and the internal ones may be, for example, thoughts, feelings or mental images.

- These experiences are fully accepted with no attempt to pass judgement on them.

- An individual's experience is to be accepted freely with an attitude of compassion towards it.

- There should be an attitude of curiosity and openness towards experience.

- Whenever one's mind wanders into daydreaming or fantasies, it should be brought back to the experience of the present.

Mindfulness-based approaches have been used to help in stress reduction, anxiety, depression and drug addiction. Many, however, would have reservations about the

Buddhist origins, the centre of focus on the self, and some aspects of non-judgemental acceptance.

How can Cognitive Behaviour Therapy (CBT) help?

CBT is based on the following:

- There is always a thought that comes before the feeling.

- These thoughts are usually unnoticed and go unchallenged.

- The thoughts are generally incorrect.

- If the thoughts are changed the feeling gets better.

CBT helps a person deal with anxiety-provoking thoughts and behaviour patterns, such as avoidance of certain situations. It can prove very valuable for those who are struggling with anxiety and panic. The person can be helped to face the anxiety-provoking situation, often with a therapist accompanying them. This behavioural measure is often extremely helpful. The therapist can explain how anxiety may affect the mind and the body, and how it can affect relationships.

People can then be taught ways of dealing with anxiety-provoking thoughts. For example, in a panic situation a person might say to themselves, 'I am going to faint.' This was the thought that was bothering Ruth, and was why she no longer wanted to visit the local supermarket.

However, this thought, 'I am going to faint', could be looked at differently. One might gently encourage the person to do some deep breathing techniques or other kind of relaxation, and then face the situation. The person then makes the discovery that they do not actually faint in that feared situation. The thought that they were going to faint has been successfully challenged. This helps the person to regain a sense of control. They begin to believe that they can now face similar situations, and once again cope with them.

How can exposure to problems help us?

Another technique that can help with anxiety problems and particularly phobias is to expose a person to the circumstances that provoked the anxiety. For example, housebound people with agoraphobia may be encouraged to go out a little further each day. This can often be done very helpfully with the aid of a therapist. The exposure is often gradual, but it can sometimes be done more rapidly if the person is able to cope with the larger degree of stress that this approach engenders. In this situation, sometimes called flooding, a person can be left in a situation which would cause intense stress. For example, a person with a phobia of spiders could be left in a room with many spiders. One finds that actually the anxiety level goes very high for a period of time (about half an hour) but after that it gradually reduces, since the body is not able to sustain a high degree of stress for long periods. If the person can cope with that degree of stress, then they might improve quite quickly. However, this is a rather unusual technique and not widely practised. Gradual exposure techniques are more commonly used, and are often combined with methods of relaxation.

Can problem-solving techniques be helpful?

Writing down a problem, and then examining it to find appropriate solutions, can be useful. Then, if nothing can be done to solve the problem, it is often best to leave it.

We also may need to help people resolve interpersonal difficulties. Interpersonal therapy can help people to examine their relationships and resolve the problems in those relationships.

What medications can help?

Medication can sometimes be useful in anxiety. SSRIs (Specific Serotonin Re-uptake Inhibitors) are often very valuable. These are best used when combined with other therapies. With anxiety, it is often best to use psychological measures and relaxation measures before one uses medication. Drugs such as Valium can be valuable where extreme anxiety is a problem. However, the problem with Valium and similar drugs is that they can induce dependence, and therefore should be given ideally only in short courses. Valium may be given on an 'as required' basis, and this can be reasonable. Other drugs are sometimes used as well.

[1] The Yerkes–Dodson curve:
http://searchpp.com/yerkes-dodson-human-performance-curve/
(accessed 3rd September 2015).
[2] Mental Health Foundation Statistics: Anxiety:
www.mentalhealth.org.uk (accessed 2nd September 2015).
[3] J. Kabat-Zinn, *Coming To Our Senses: Healing Ourselves and the World Through Mindfulness* (New York, Hyperion, 2005).

Recommended resources

Anxiety UK (helping to support those living with anxiety): www.anxietyuk.org.uk (accessed 4th September 2015).

No Panic (helping you break the chains of anxiety disorders): www.nopanic.org.uk (helpline: 0844 967 4848; youth helpline: 01753 840393) (accessed 4th September 2015).

FearFighter (Online CBT – can be prescribed by your doctor): www.fearfighter.com (temporary website; accessed 4th September 2015).

Chapter two
Spiritual help in stress and anxiety

So far we have discussed anxiety and stress in purely medical and psychological terms. However, we are spiritual beings, and there is a spiritual side to this problem. As a Christian, I find the teachings of Jesus Christ to be invaluable, and also the Psalms, which are found in the Old Testament. I sometimes encourage people to use Psalm 23 as a way of expressing our dependence on God.

Psalm 23 starts with the statement: 'The Lord is my shepherd, I lack nothing.' This is inspiring. To know that God can be our shepherd to guide and lead and provide for us makes the whole of life worth living.

The next verse tells us: 'He makes me lie down in green pastures, he leads me beside quiet waters'. These words are comforting and helpful because they talk about our relationship with God and the rest He gives.

The psalm also goes on to tell us that 'he refreshes my soul. He guides me along the right paths for his name's sake.' That is a promise of guidance and restoration and refreshment in our lives.

It then continues, 'Even though I walk through the darkest valley, I will fear no evil, for you are with me; your rod and your staff, they comfort me.' Again, this can be most uplifting for people going through very difficult and traumatic times in their lives.

'You prepare a table before me in the presence of my enemies' reminds us that when everything seems against us, God's presence is still with us.

'You anoint my head with oil; my cup overflows. Surely your goodness and love will follow me all the days of my life, and I will dwell in the house of the Lord for ever.' There is joy in knowing God's blessing on our lives. We can know that God will never leave us, and we can anticipate an eternity in His presence.

Learning to meditate on a psalm like this can be very helpful.

In the last chapter, I discussed the concept of Mindfulness. Fernando Garzon,[1] writing for the Society for Christian Psychology in 2011, points out major differences between Mindfulness and Christian Devotional Meditation. In Mindfulness, there are emphases on the self with increasing self-awareness, acceptance and compassion towards the self. In Christian Devotional Meditation, the emphases are on God and the Scriptures as well as the self, with awareness both of oneself and God. There is confidence in God and experience of His grace, alongside confession and surrender to Him.

Learning to live more in the present is an aspect of both Mindfulness and Christian Devotional Meditation. This can be important for us. Near my home is a three-mile beautiful walk which takes me around a golf course and then along a riverbank. As I walked today, I was aware of the lovely sunny morning, of the rabbits on the path scampering to safety, of the cows and calf in the field, and was glad of the beautiful day and the strength in my limbs. This increased awareness led me to give thanks to my Creator.

In his book entitled, *A Book of Sparks – A Study in Christian Mindfullness*,[2] the author, Shaun Lambert, takes us on a journey of exploration to show how we can experience more of God in our lives. (Note the change in spelling to denote the anticipation that we would know more of God's fullness.) The desire of the apostle Paul was that we might be 'filled to the measure of all the fullness of God' (Ephesians 3:19). Shaun Lambert discusses two methods of Christian meditation that can help us along the way. The first of these is a simple but profound prayer, which is a combination of prayers prayed by a tax collector and a blind beggar as recorded in the Gospel of Luke, chapter 18. It is called the 'Jesus Prayer' and has been in use since the fifth century as a prayer that can be repeated many times, meditatively, as a way of coming into God's presence.

The prayer is: 'Lord Jesus Christ, Son of God, have mercy on me, a sinner.'

The second meditative practice, called 'Lectio Divina', is a way of reading biblical passages very slowly and using the scripture as a foundation for prayer. The same passage could be used over several days and perhaps memorised. Psalm 23, as above, can be used in this way.

These simple exercises in meditation can help us slow down and come into the living presence of Almighty God.

The teaching of Christ on anxiety is extremely helpful. For example, we read words like these:

> Therefore I tell you, do not worry about your life, what you will eat or drink; or about your body, what you will wear. Is not life more than food, and the body more than clothes? Look at the birds of the air; they do not sow or reap or store away in barns, and yet your heavenly Father feeds them. Are you not much more valuable than they? Can any one of you by worrying add a single hour to your life?
> *Matthew 6:25–27*

Jesus is clearly teaching us here that we have a heavenly Father who is concerned about us. We do not need to worry or become anxious because God is looking after us, in the details of our lives.

I went to Cyprus in 1990 with my wife and daughters, and we lived there for six years. For two and a half years, I was not practising medically but rather was leading a church. During my time there, we had an experience where we completely ran out of money. I just had a few coins left in my pocket. I needed to feed my wife and family, and this was my responsibility.

I clearly remember going to the local Cypriot supermarket one day. It was just before the Greek Orthodox celebration of Easter, and at that time of year many Cypriots stopped eating meat. In response, the shopkeepers raised the price of vegetables. So I was a little stuck; I wanted to buy some cauliflowers, but they were far too expensive for me. I remember standing in the shop, praying to my heavenly Father that He would give me cauliflowers because I needed to feed my family. I knew that I had some cheese to put with them, which was in the fridge at home. However, I had to leave the shop disappointed, because I did not have sufficient money. Imagine my surprise when I opened the kitchen door and found three great big cauliflowers in addition to a lot of other vegetables on the table in front of me. How could this have happened?

I realised that this was God's way of showing me that He was with us, and would support us and help us in every situation we faced. However, I was still mystified as to how the vegetables had arrived there. I knew that my wife had done some babysitting for a family in our church who had a market garden. It transpired that the husband had felt that morning that he should bring vegetables round to our house for us. This was a clear answer to prayer and confirmation that God was looking after us. Similarly, in the following week on three separate days great big bags of food, including all kinds of meat, arrived outside our back door. On the third occasion, I saw a man beating a hasty retreat. It was someone with whom I had had a number of recent discussions. Again, we had not shared our needs with him. God was looking after us.

The crisis passed, and we had enough money, but I always knew after this that God indeed was my heavenly Father and would provide for me. Jesus, in the above passage from the Gospel of Matthew, was reminding His disciples that God was their heavenly Father. He reminds us, too, that we do not need to worry about the body and clothing and physical things because God will provide for us. However, He also adds in this passage, 'But seek first his kingdom and his righteousness, and all these things will be given to you as well' (Matthew 6:33). This passage, like the rest of this section (commonly called the Sermon on the Mount), is primarily written for those who are disciples who, in Christ's terms, are seeking His kingdom and His righteousness.

Christ ends this section by saying:

Therefore do not worry about tomorrow, for tomorrow will worry about itself. Each day has enough trouble of its own.
Matthew 6:34

Jesus is telling us to live one day at a time and not to worry about the future. This does not mean that we should not plan for the future. However, fruitless worry will be of no use to us, and as Jesus said, we cannot add an hour to our life by worrying.

In the book of 1 Peter, we read these words:

Humble yourselves, therefore, under God's mighty hand, that he may lift you up in due time. Cast all your anxiety on him because he cares for you.
1 Peter 5:6–7

There is a clear command here. First, there is the need to humble ourselves under God's mighty hand. The promise is not to everyone, but to those who humble themselves before God. Pride is seen in the Bible as something that is related to independence, and independence from God is something that He hates. He wants us to humble ourselves in His presence so that we can receive from His goodness and grace. However, having humbled ourselves in His presence, we can then cast all of our cares upon Him because He cares for us.

How does this apply to our lives? Well, first of all, writing down all of our anxieties and problems can be a helpful exercise. We can then examine the list before us, and decide what we can do about the problems we have listed. There may be some effective measures we can take to resolve some of the anxiety-provoking issues. However, there will be other issues that we cannot deal with. What do we do about these? We pass them on to God. Sometimes it can be helpful to actually screw the paper up and throw it, and say, 'God, take these problems because I cannot deal with them.'

If God tells us to cast our cares upon Him, then we can expect that He will gently show us the answers to our problems. This may not be immediate, but we can now be at rest, knowing that God will help us with our difficulties. This is what it means to cast all of our cares upon Him, because He cares about us.

I have found this to be a very helpful exercise. Many years ago, as a new consultant in psychiatry, I found that I had many anxiety-provoking issues at the end of the day. I would write these down and decide what I could do about them. I found that there were some issues I could deal with then and there, but beyond that I would leave the rest with God. And then I would relax and enjoy the evening.

Other verses that are very helpful in helping us to deal with anxiety are these, where Paul writes to the church of Philippi, saying:

Do not be anxious about anything, but in every situation, by prayer and petition, with thanksgiving, present your requests to God. And the peace of God, which transcends all understanding, will guard your hearts and your minds in Christ Jesus.
Philippians 4:6–7

Here Paul is saying that prayer is very important. If we are feeling anxious, he tells us to pray. And he tells us to pray earnestly, with petition. In our prayer, we are giving God our problems. Paul says we are to pray until the peace of God fills our hearts and minds in Christ Jesus. I have often found this advice to be helpful. In a situation where I felt anxious and experienced a lack of peace, I found I could bring the issue to God in prayer, and I could pour out my heart before God and know that He heard me. After a while, although I did not know the answer to the problem, I had the sense that God had heard about the issue, and that He would indeed show me the relevant answer.

These promises of God can be very helpful in anxiety. In each of the above three passages of Scripture, God promises us His help when we face anxiety-provoking situations. However, this does imply that we, first of all, must have a clear relationship with God as our Father. How can we make sure we have such a relationship as this?

This is what Jesus says:

Come to me, all you who are weary and burdened, and I will give you rest. Take my yoke upon you and learn from me, for I am gentle and humble in heart, and you will find rest for your souls. For my yoke is easy and my burden is light.
Matthew 11:28–30

In this passage, Jesus is telling us how we can have a relationship with Him. First of all, there is the instruction to come to Him. This is simple, but it is very important. We are inclined to try to solve all of our relationship and other difficulties by ourselves. However, if we are to have a real relationship with God, then we must drop our pride and come to Christ in humility. We should say, 'Yes, Lord, I am coming to You. I want to learn from You and follow You.' Jesus then tells us that if we will do this, then we will find rest for our souls. How can we find this rest? Again, Jesus tells us clearly, using an agricultural analogy. Imagine there are two oxen trying to plough a field. If the oxen are not joined together, they will go in different directions, and the furrow in the field will be far from straight. However, if the oxen are joined together at the neck by a yoke, then they will be going in the same direction, and the furrow will be straight. Jesus is saying here that He wants us to be yoked together with Him. If we are yoked together with Jesus, what does that mean? It means essentially that I have given up my own independence. I am not trying any longer to live life purely for myself by my own willpower and good intentions. I am not trying to please God in my own strength. What I have said, instead, is, 'I am willing to come to You, Jesus and be yoked together with You, and we will walk the course of life together.'

Imagine you are the driver of a car. However, you are not a very good driver, and you have had many accidents. That is rather like our lives without Christ. We find that trying to drive our own lives can lead us into many disasters. Our lives may be in a terrible mess. We can recognise the mistakes we have made. Even when we try to live with the best intentions, things have gone wrong and difficult relationships and other issues have had a major impact upon us.

What is the answer to this situation? It is to have somebody else in the driving seat. This does not mean that we do not plan or think carefully about our lives, but it does mean that we give our wills to Jesus Christ and say, 'Jesus, I want Your plan for my life, not my own.' It is effectively handing over the car keys to Jesus. It is saying, 'Jesus, You be the number one in my life. You lead me and guide me, and I will follow You.' Jesus, when He called His disciples, called them to follow Him.

He said, 'I am the light of the world. Whoever follows me will never walk in darkness, but will have the light of life' (John 8:12). This is what it really means to be a Christian. A Christian is somebody who is yoked together with Jesus, who now says, 'I will follow you, Lord.'

If we do this, then the furrow in the field will be straight. We will be going in the same direction as Jesus. We will find His power and His presence in our lives. Again I emphasise these words of Jesus:

Take my yoke upon you and learn from me, for I am gentle and humble in heart, and you will find rest for your souls. For my yoke is easy and my burden is light.
Matthew 11:29–30

If we follow Him, we will find rest in Him.

Summary of chapters one and two

- Anxiety is a common problem.

- It can affect our minds, bodies and relationships.

- There are a number of practical measures that can prove helpful.

- Learning methods of stress reduction can be very important for us.

- The Bible has much practical advice to give us.

- Developing a real relationship with Jesus Christ is vitally important.

---

[1] 'Mindfulness and Christian Devotional Meditation', Fernando Garzon, Society for Christian Psychology, August 2011: www.christianpsych.org (accessed 8th September 2015).
[2] Shaun Lambert, *A Book of Sparks: A Study in Christian MindFullness* (Watford, Instant Apostle, 2014).

Chapter three
The person with depression

Depression affects many people. One lady explained that she was putting the children to bed and was reading a bedtime story. She carried on reading and read the same passage three times before she realised that she could not finish the story. She decided she needed to see a doctor the next day. She was struggling with difficulties in concentration.

Another lady said that she felt as though she was in the middle of a very thick balloon, and the harder she tried to push out against it, the skin of the balloon pushed her back in. She was expressing what many people feel about depression. She felt trapped and there seemed no way out.

Cathy Wield, in her book *A Thorn in My Mind*,[1] describes her depression in these terms:

I felt so low, the darkness was almost tangible. I kept myself shut in the bedroom except when the children came home from school ... The initial tears had dried up and my emotions went numb apart from a growing fear and anxiety that I was never going to get out of this. The once rosy future looked grey and ugly as indeed my life had become. I was forever tired and had no energy;

even normal movements felt heavy and protracted, described aptly as though 'wading through treacle'. Despite the absolute fatigue, I could not sleep ... My thoughts took on a life of their own; I was a complete failure, I had brought this on myself, I was a bad person.

Other people describe depression as being like a black cloud over them. Winston Churchill named it his 'Black Dog'. Many other famous leaders have struggled with depression. Abraham Lincoln, the sixteenth President of the United States, suffered from severe and debilitating suicidal depression. The most amazing part of his story was the sheer determination with which he willed himself to overcome serious depression and still accomplish all he was able to achieve for the young and troubled nation of America, at war with itself.

Vincent van Gogh, the famous artist, had unstable moods for most of his short life. He also suffered from epileptic seizures. His depressive states were accompanied by manic episodes of enormous energy and great passion. He died by suicide at the age of 37. Beethoven had bipolar disorder, which some said gave him tremendous creative power. His compositions broke the mould in classical music forever. His manic episodes seemed to fuel his creativity.

Alastair Campbell was the right-hand man of Tony Blair, previous Prime Minister of the United Kingdom. Campbell told Blair about his breakdown, alcohol problem and depression. However, Tony Blair was understanding and was able to tell him that his problems were no barrier to their working relationship. Similarly, Catherine Zeta-Jones, the actress, received treatment for bipolar disorder after dealing with the stress of her husband's battle with cancer. She made a decision to check into a mental health facility for a brief stay.

How does depression affect us?

Richard, a single man aged 59, walked down the corridor towards the office. I had met him several times before. He had suffered from serious depression a few years before after a heart attack, but since then he had generally been doing fine. He had been a foreman in a local factory, and I had heard that the factory had closed down around four months ago, but I had not seen Richard since then. He was a keen supporter of the local football team and enjoyed going out for a pint at the local pub on Saturday nights with a few friends. However, today I sensed something was wrong. He was walking slowly and looking at the floor. In response to my cheery 'Good morning!' he barely mumbled a reply.

When he sat down in the office, he kept looking down. I noticed several days' stubble on his chin, and his jacket was food-stained. His hands were grimy, and I thought I could sense a slightly stale body odour. I asked him how he was, and after a long pause with no response, asked him the question again.

Eventually he replied. He still did not look at me properly, and his voice was so low it was hard to make him out. 'Not good, doctor,' was what he appeared to say. I noticed his trousers were a bit loose on him, as if he had lost weight recently.

Again there was a long pause. I decided to ask a few general questions to try to get the conversation going. How was his favourite football team doing?

'Don't know,' was the simple reply.

I asked him about the friends he met at the pub. He had not seen them for some time.

'Life is very difficult,' was all he could say. 'I worked in the factory for 30 years, and now it's all gone. Redundant.'

I explained how sorry I was to hear this news. I asked if he had been eating properly.

'No appetite, doctor,' he said.

'How are you sleeping?'

'Can't sleep,' he said. 'Upset about losing the job.'

I gently persisted. 'Are you going out at all?'

'Can't be bothered,' he said. 'I just sit there, and gaze out of the window.'

'How long have you been feeling like this?'

'Every day. It's worse in the mornings. I'm low and down all the time. Can't seem to shake myself out of it,' he added.

He thought he had probably lost about a stone in weight. Also, he had been on Citalopram, an antidepressant, but had stopped taking it around six months previously, because he had felt so well then. He said he couldn't concentrate well enough to read. He read the same thing two or three times and then gave up.

I gently asked how low he was actually feeling.

'Very low,' he said. 'Sometimes I feel as though I don't want to carry on.'

I asked him if he had had any thoughts of harming himself.

'No,' he said. 'I would never harm myself. Might have had an occasional thought, but I would never do anything to myself.'

I asked him what would actually stop him, and he added, 'Well, my nephew has two young boys, and I could never do anything to hurt my nephew and his wee boys.'

Although I was concerned about him, he did say this quite convincingly, and he had never tried to harm himself in the past.

I expressed my concerns about his eating and his degree of social isolation. He agreed to restart the Citalopram. I told him that I would like to refer him to a psychiatric nurse who would call and see him several times in the coming few weeks. I also arranged to see him myself for review in just two weeks.

After he left the office, I rang Mark, the community psychiatric nurse, and explained that Richard would need careful review over the next few weeks. I asked Mark if he could try to encourage Richard to eat properly and to ensure he took his medication correctly. I also asked if he could help him towards more social involvement. Mark was a good listener and very sensitive, and I was quite relieved he could see Richard the next day. I assured him that he could ring me if he had any concerns.

Depression is common. It is twice as frequent in women as it is in men.[2] One man in ten requires treatment for depression at some time during his life. This compares with one woman in four. Although depression is much more common in women, death by suicide is much more common in men.[3] British men are around three times as likely to die by suicide as women.

One question raised by these figures is this. Depression is a major cause of suicide. How is it, then, that the depression rate is twice as high in women, yet the suicide rate is three times as high in men? One of the reasons for this is that men will often hide their feelings. Rather than talking about their problems they will tend to keep their difficulties to themselves. They may see a doctor for a physical health issue, but will be reluctant to open up about feelings of low mood and depression. Instead they may take their problems down to the local pub and drink to try to alleviate them.

Drinking alcohol instead of dealing with problems is extremely dangerous. There are three main dangers of taking alcohol as a way of dealing with mental health issues.

- Firstly, many people do not realise that alcohol is, in fact, a depressant. Many people who drink will become more depressed following the alcohol. I remember several patients coming to a ward on which I was the doctor. They were often quite seriously depressed. However, following the enforced abstinence from alcohol, they began to improve spontaneously, without the need for further treatment.

- Secondly, those who take alcohol as a way of dealing with mental health issues are more likely to suffer from dependency as a result.

- Thirdly, alcohol may make people much more impulsive. People are more likely to harm themselves or die by suicide following taking alcohol when they are depressed. Suicide statistics show that approximately one-third of people who have died by suicide have taken alcohol.[4]

Knowing these problems with alcohol, I was quite relieved to find that Richard had not turned to drink to try to help himself; instead, as he had been going out very little, he had, in fact, stopped drinking at this time.

What is depression?

Many people regard depression as just feeling a little low or a little 'blue'. However, this is not true depression. To ascertain whether a person is depressed, I find it helpful to ask two key questions. It is important to establish how much of the time the person is feeling low and depressed.

I will ask them, for example, for how many days in the last two weeks they have felt low and depressed for most of the day. If the answer is one or two days, this leads to relatively less concern. However, should the answer be at least seven days or more, then I would be much more concerned. In Richard's case, he had been feeling very low in mood every day and all day long over the last few weeks.

The second key question I ask is whether the person is finding any enjoyment from activities that they usually find pleasurable. People with severe depression will tend to lose interest in the things that they usually enjoy. For example, somebody who enjoyed playing golf or going for a walk may have no longer any interest in these activities. This is a warning sign. Richard showed no interest in his favourite football team, and he had no motivation to leave the house.

The appearance of the individual may point towards depression. A person may look depressed and may gaze at the floor, avoiding eye contact. There may be marked slowness of movement. Richard had shown all these signs. This is what had alerted me to the fact that something was wrong even as he was walking down the corridor to my office. The eyes may appear sad. The corners of the mouth may be downturned. There may be a general air of depression. The voice might be low in tone, with a lack of modulation as in normal speech. The appearance may be unkempt and untidy. A person may be slow in their thought processes.

In depression, bodily systems are also affected. I can recall seeing one man brought into hospital, who had been living alone. When he came into hospital he was so thin that his bones were protruding. He had not been eating and drinking properly for some time and had lost a massive amount of weight. He needed urgent treatment. He had no medical illness. His condition was simply due to severe depression.

Richard had also lost considerable weight, and his sleeping had become very poor. The sleep pattern is usually affected in depression. Often a person will wake up early in the morning and at this time morbid thoughts might be going through the mind more than at other times of the day. There may be a feeling that life is not worth living. Concentration is often very poor. Anxiety may be present. Sometimes there may be a complaint of poor memory. When one is depressed and fails to concentrate properly, the memory may be affected. Sometimes a person with depression may appear very agitated. This is often true of older people. Many times the person will have little energy and feel tired all the time. A sense of guilt may be present. The guilt experienced in depression is often a false guilt.

For example, I remember one man who complained that he was the worst person in the world. When I asked him further about this, he said that he had made a mistake on his income tax forms 20 years before. This made him the worst person in the world. I enquired more carefully to find out how fixed his belief was. When asked to clarify the statement, he insisted that he was the worst person in the world because he had made this mistake. He suffered from an unshakeable belief, which was a depressive delusion. On the other hand, another man I met shortly after that had led a fine, upstanding life, until on one occasion during a business trip abroad, he had slept with a woman other than his wife. He felt very upset about what had happened and could not forgive himself. One might argue that his guilt was real, and had been a factor in his profound depression.

Feeling worthless is often a feature of depression. Self-esteem can be very low. This can lead to an extremely low mood. Together with this, there may be thoughts of death or suicide.

If someone is seriously depressed, it is very important to ask about suicidal thoughts or tendencies. However, this needs to be done carefully. It is usually a mistake to ask this question too soon in the interview. One first needs to build a rapport with the person and try to empathise with them in their difficulties. Then is the time to ask gently how the person is feeling. One might sensitively ask about the future or whether life is worth living. This can then be followed up with questions about thoughts of self-harm and enquiries as to the presence of actual thoughts of suicide. If these thoughts are present, it is important to ask further questions to elucidate whether any plans have been made. The risk of suicide is much more likely in those who have definite suicidal plans, rather than those who have suicidal thoughts without plans.

In Richard's case, I was relieved that he denied suicidal thoughts and I felt fairly confident that he was telling me the truth. If he had been suicidal, since he had such little social support, I might have had to admit him to hospital.

The risks have to be very carefully assessed. In reality, assessment is not easy since sometimes a person may not reveal the precise nature of their thoughts. Most practising psychiatrists will have had one or two patients who have died by suicide. It is often unexpected when people actually take their own lives. If they had been open about the true nature of their thoughts and feelings, might the outcomes have been different?

What is the difference between unipolar and bipolar depression?

In mental health we generally make a distinction between what we call unipolar and bipolar depression. Unipolar depression, when it occurs, tends to present in a similar way to that described above. There is low mood, lack of energy, poor motivation, reduced appetite and disturbed sleep. Richard has this type of depression. The way he presented this time was similar to the previous time, although this time it was worse.

Manic depression or bipolar disorder is rather different. In this, there are usually depressive episodes which are severe; however, there are other periods where the individual tends to become elated or irritable in mood. In the high, or manic phase, a person may become very disturbed. There are different grades, and some people may become extremely high and manic whereas others are less severe. We tend to distinguish between Bipolar 1, which is when true mania is present, and Bipolar 2, where there is a lower degree of mania or hypomania present. In hypomania the person may be excitable or irritable with disturbed sleep and racing thoughts but without the full manic picture.

In the full-blown manic state many things may happen. The thoughts are racing and there might be grandiose ideas present (exaggerated beliefs of one's own importance); for example, there might be plans to change the world or begin a major, fresh business venture that cannot, in the eyes of someone in this state, possibly fail. They may have stopped sleeping completely. They may be rushing around in a heightened state of arousal. They might not dress properly, or might have a bizarre or highly colourful style of dress. They can run around half-dressed, or behave in other very inappropriate ways, placing their reputations seriously at risk. They can waste all their money on some new enterprise. Their speech is often disorganised, and they may make strange associations between one sentence and the next. They may start a new sentence with a word rhyming with that which closed the last sentence. For example, 'I went to the shop. Hop on the bus.' They can be very difficult to deal with, as they typically have absolutely no insight into their condition. They feel they are normal: however, those around them know that this is far from the case. Sometimes they are aggressive and highly irritable.

People in this much-heightened state of arousal need rapid medical care. They will need medication and they will often need to be in hospital for a period of time, to allow them to calm down sufficiently to carry on with normal life. If they are left to their own devices, then they may rapidly become exhausted and at serious risk to their own health and safety.

What is Seasonal Affective Disorder?

Another type of depression we recognise is Seasonal Affective Disorder (SAD). In this condition, as the nights grow longer and the days grow shorter, the person is more likely to be affected. The rate tends to increase the closer one is to the North Pole. For example, in northern Scandinavia, the risk of SAD is much higher than it would be, for example, in Cyprus and Italy. In someone with SAD, it can often be predicted when the person is likely to become depressed. For example, as the nights grow longer, the depression may begin to emerge.

One way of dealing with this is by giving antidepressants before the known time of risk. Light treatment is sometimes helpful, placing the person in very bright light for certain periods of the day. The logic behind this is as follows. If loss of daylight seems to have brought on the condition, can it be reversed by giving very bright light on a daily or more frequent basis? Results from this are variable. Some people have strong confidence that light treatment is effective, while others are a little more doubtful.

Are there other types of depression?

In what is sometimes called 'atypical' depression, instead of weight loss there is weight gain, and instead of poor sleep the person might sleep excessively. In patients with dysthymia (mild but persistent low mood), the mood tends to be low for much of the time, but other features typical of depression as mentioned above tend to be absent. Depression may occur at particular stages of life and may be associated with the postnatal period. It can also complicate bereavement.

Who suffers most from depression?

Depression is more common in those who are divorced, separated or unemployed. The lonely and those who are on their own for various reasons, such as Richard, can be more vulnerable. The rate of depression in prisoners is high. Those who have seen active military service are at risk of depression. Farmers living alone in rural areas are at risk. Those with other psychiatric conditions are also vulnerable. Certain professions, including doctors, show an increased risk. Young people living away from home in bedsit accommodation are also vulnerable.

What leads to depression?

Factors related to depression can be considered in three groups.

- Firstly, there are those that are related to early life. These are genetic factors and factors related to early childhood environment.

- Secondly, there are things that happen to us that precede the onset of the illness. These may be termed 'life events'.

- Thirdly, there are factors that can tend to maintain or perpetuate the depression.

How may genetic factors and early life experiences be related to depression?

Depression is more common in some families than in others. This is in part related to genetic predisposition. If one person in a family is affected, then the risk of depression for a close family member is about twice what might be expected in the general population.

We used to believe that bipolar disease was about ten per cent as common as unipolar disease; however, more recent research would suggest that this is an underestimate.[5] The genetic link is more marked in bipolar illness than it is in unipolar. A genetic component does not mean that a person will suffer from the illness. It means, rather, that the risk of illness is slightly greater in those who have this genetic predisposition.

Childhood experience can lead to an increased risk of depression. If there is a loss of parent in childhood, or absence of parents for other reasons, such as separation or divorce, then an increased risk of depression is present. If physical or sexual abuse was experienced in childhood, then the possibility is higher. Where parents tend to be overprotective or neglectful there can also be an increased risk.

Personality is also a factor in depression. Those who have the tendency to perfectionism may not be satisfied unless they have reached perfection in a given task. They are unable to accept any lesser degree of performance. This may make life difficult, because not everything can be done perfectly. It is helpful for those with a tendency towards perfectionism to try to understand their personalities and work towards developing more realistic expectations of themselves. Those with anxious tendencies or anxious personalities can also show an increased risk of depression. There are people who tend to worry about everything. They need to understand their anxiety and discover ways of finding help for it. Those with an obsessional personality show an increased risk. As they struggle with their ongoing obsessional thought patterns they may become frustrated, exhausted and depressed. All these background factors may make depression more likely.

What factors may precede the onset of depression?

The second group of factors are life events which often occur just preceding the onset of depression. These often involve some kind of loss. For most people with depression, this loss is usually of things that are particularly important to them.

As a psychiatrist mainly working with older people, I used to find that many people who came to see me had suffered some kind of major loss in the few months before; for example, there were those who had become extremely depressed following the loss of their spouse. Some people are quite unable to carry on a normal life following the death of someone with whom they had been very close for many years. Other causes are related to loss of health. They may be unable to cope with the stress of illness, such as diabetes or loss of eyesight, stroke, Parkinson's disease, cancer, or other serious illness. The loss may be financial. In the recent economic downturn, there has been quite a large rise in the suicide rate in many developed nations. The losses created by unemployment, home repossessions and other economic difficulties have had major impacts on people's lives. In some, their closest relationship can be with their pet, and when the pet dies this can be a huge loss for them. Any of these loss events can make depression more likely.

Other people may experience many life changes over a brief period of time. For example, there may be a new job. There may be a change of housing. Too much is happening at the same time, and some people cannot cope with a rapid pace of change.

Depression can sometimes occur without an apparent reason. At times, someone will be in hospital with severe depression but it can prove very difficult or impossible to elucidate the contributory factors.

What factors tend to perpetuate or maintain depression?

As well as 'loss' events, it is important to recognise the role of ongoing problems as factors in depression. People may feel trapped in situations which seem difficult or impossible to resolve. For example, a woman with young children at home may be unable to go out and find a job, or pursue other interests. In this situation, if the woman concerned has a confidante that she can share with, then there can potentially be improvement. However, the woman might not know anyone with whom she can really share. This can increase the likelihood of depression.

These, and similar unresolved and ongoing problems in people's lives, can be factors both in the onset of depression and in its maintenance once it has occurred.

What are the risks of recurrence of depression once it has been treated?

If one has a serious depressive episode, the risk of having a further one is high. As many as two-thirds of people who have suffered depression may have a further bout at some stage.[6] It is usually possible to recover from an episode of depression. However, prevention of a further bout can be difficult, particularly if the person does not make a complete recovery, or fails to adhere to the treatment plan, which will commonly involve taking an antidepressant. If there have been several episodes of depression, the risk of further depression continues to increase. In my practice, I used to find that some older people were depressed all the time, despite valiant attempts at a cure. No matter what treatment is prescribed, some ten per cent of people will remain depressed, and this is more likely with older people.

What are the chemical changes in the body in depression?

Noradrenaline and serotonin, naturally occurring chemicals in the brain, are believed, along with other substances, to be implicated in depression. Antidepressants tend to raise the levels of either one or both of these substances at nerve endings.

Hormones are also instrumental in the process of depression, particularly a hormone called cortisol. Early life events seem to have subtle effects on the brain which, when triggered by recent events, can affect cortisol, noradrenaline and serotonin.

How can we help the person with depression?

One of the key factors in prevention or improvement regarding depression is being able to talk about one's feelings. In the case of Richard, he had talked to no one about the way he was feeling since he had been made redundant. Even when he came to the clinic, it was quite difficult to get him to talk about his experiences. When someone is depressed, it can be helpful just to be there and available for that person. In a gentle and encouraging way, but never forcibly, we want to try to help someone talk about their problems. This can be really beneficial. As the person may have stopped eating and sleeping properly, encouragement of normal routines in these areas can be very important. The family can often help with this.

People with depression may withdraw socially, and it is not unusual for them to wish to stay alone in their rooms for long hours at a time. Encouraging some form of social interaction can be very important. This might be at a day centre for an older person, or encouraging and helping a younger person to be involved in group activities, if at all possible. However, someone who is very severely depressed may be unwilling to engage in this way, and attempts at coercion will often be unfruitful.

Exercise is beneficial in depression and other forms of mental illness. Group exercises are particularly valuable. We want to help the person with depression to remain involved in life and not to withdraw. We also want to encourage them to stay off alcohol and addictive drugs. These can lead to dependency problems and erratic behaviour, and can make the depression worse. We should also be aware of the risk of suicide and be unafraid to ask about this. Sometimes a person may be unwilling to see a doctor because of feelings of depression, or the stigma associated with mental illness, but perhaps may be willing to accept a review for associated physical problems. For example, if a person's appetite is poor, or they are losing weight, then they can be encouraged to see the doctor for these problems, even if they are unwilling to see the doctor for depression.

In terms of helping people with depression, it is also important that we do not blame them and say that they should not be depressed. This does not help and only adds blame to the depression. Also, we should not say to the person, 'Pull yourself together.' If people could pull themselves together, they would have done this by now!

How important is a medical opinion?

A medical opinion when one is seriously depressed is important. There are several reasons for this.

- Firstly, and importantly, the doctor will be in the best position to assess the depth of depression. For example, somebody with very severe depression may need urgent help, whereas with a milder form of depression the need may be less urgent.

- Secondly, the doctor may also be in a position to be able to ascertain if there are underlying factors related to the depression. These might be physical, psychological, sociological and spiritual in varying combinations particular to each individual. (Spiritual factors may not be recognised by all, and there is further discussion of these factors in the next chapter.) Underlying physical illness may be present. For example, people with hormonal imbalances of cortisol or thyroxine can suffer from depression. Depression can follow influenza or hepatitis. The doctor can assess the person and arrange tests to exclude physical illness.

- Thirdly, the doctor can then decide on a treatment plan. This may involve prescribing antidepressants and possibly a course of CBT or similar. Occasionally, Electro-Convulsive Therapy (ECT) can still be used for those who have very severe depression or are very suicidal, or where the depression does not respond to any other measures. Although ECT has had a bad press, when one takes into account its effectiveness in saving the lives of people who are extremely depressed, it still has its place in treatment. Maintaining a healthy normal diet, as far as possible, is also important. Although there has been some debate about the issue, it is likely that certain fish oils, minerals and B vitamins can be beneficial.

For how long should one take antidepressants?

Antidepressants can be very valuable. Sometimes a person may not respond well initially. It is important to ensure that the medication is being taken as prescribed. There is usually a time lag of around two weeks before the person begins to respond.

There may be a need to try more than one antidepressant to find one that suits the individual and to which the person responds. Antidepressants do have some side effects but these are usually tolerable. They are not addictive, although with some there can be a withdrawal reaction, particularly if they are stopped too suddenly. An antidepressant is given with the aim of helping the depression resolve, and is then continued for a variable period of time following this, to prevent recurrence. If a person has had several bouts of depression, then the antidepressant may be continued longer term, and other drugs may also be given to aid recovery. In an acute situation with poor sleep, a sedative may be given on a short-term basis. In bipolar illness, mood stabilisers such as Lithium may be needed, and alternative mood stabilisers are available.

How can Cognitive Behaviour Therapy (CBT) help?

This has value in a range of mental health conditions, and particularly in depression. Behavioural measures can be beneficial. People with depression may be reluctant to be socially involved and may stay in their rooms with little motivation and interest. Helping to motivate a person to do simple activities can be very valuable. Some of these activities might be planned to give a sense of achievement – like today, a person managed to wash the dishes. Other activities might be planned around something that the person previously enjoyed, such as watching a film or going for a walk. Even though the person might not want to try to do these things, if they can be so persuaded, then the simple carrying out of these planned activities can be therapeutic.

Engaging the help of a family member in the planning of such activities can prove helpful. These changes may help prepare the person to then be able to engage with the process of examining their thought patterns.

In depression, the thoughts are often very negative but may be incorrect. For example, if I breeze into the office and greet my secretary and receive no response, I might be very concerned. I could easily imagine that she is upset with me over something I had done. I might carry this negative thought with me throughout the day and as a result feel miserable. However, if I asked my secretary why she had not greeted me, I might find that she had not heard me or that she had been totally distracted with another problem. Then I would realise that her non-response had nothing to do with me, and I would consequently be relieved and enjoy the day.

People with depression often make similar mistakes in their thinking. If these thoughts can be successfully challenged, then they can be significantly helped. But while CBT has been shown to be very valuable in depression, a person with very severe depression may not be well enough to engage in the process.

Which other therapies may be beneficial?

Interpersonal therapy aimed at helping people work through their relationship difficulties, can be instrumental in recovery for some people. Family therapy, bereavement counselling, couple therapy, and problem-solving therapy can all have their place, either for the individual person or together in groups, but the use of various therapies will often depend on the stage of the illness. If a person is very unwell with depression, they may be unable to derive much benefit from these therapies, which are usually more valuable when the person has recovered to an extent.

In what ways can we help a person at risk from depression?

Talking through problems before they become severe can be very helpful.

If loss of finances or employment are factors, then proper advice and help may be available to deal with these issues. Likewise, support and help may be found for ongoing social problems. Attention to possible underlying physical illness may be necessary. Adherence to medication and treatment plans can be vital. At a proper time and with skilled help, deeper issues, such as childhood problems, may be addressed (but not during an acute illness).

Are religious factors important in mental health and depression?

In answer to this, I want to consider briefly a paper on 'The psychosocial benefits of religious practice' by Professor Patricia Casey of Dublin.[7] She reports on an analysis of more than 300 research papers which discuss the interconnections between mental health and religious practice. She emphasises the importance of religious practice rather than religious belief or spirituality. She finds a positive connection between religious practice and mental health. Other authors have shown similar findings.[8] These positive findings may be seen in six particular areas:

- Those who regularly practise their religious faith are found to have less depression.

- There is also less suicide.

- They are also found to live longer.

- Their marriages hold together better.

- Young people do better in terms of reduced levels of drug and alcohol abuse and other risky behaviour.

- People who practise their religion regularly cope better with bereavement.

Patricia Casey argues that if enough people in society practise their religious faith, then the benefits will accrue to the whole of society. She is saying that there will be a societal benefit as a result of regular religious practice.

These findings are important and worthy of better recognition.

---

[1] Cathy Wield, *A Thorn in My Mind* (Watford, Instant Apostle, 2012), pp. 29–30.

[2] Depression Alliance: Mental Health Foundation Mental Health Statistics: Men and Women: www.mentalhealth.org.uk (accessed 3rd September 2015).

[3] Samaritans: suicide statistics report www.samaritans.org/sites/default/.../Suicide_statistics_report_2 015 Page 6 (accessed 3rd September 2015).

[4] A. Ohberg, E.Vuori, I. Ojanperä, et al, 'Alcohol and drugs in suicides', *British Journal of Psychiatry*, 169:75-8 (1996).

[5] Bipolar Disorder Among Adults: www.nimh.nih.gov (accessed 3rd September 2015)

[6] D. A. Solomon, M. B. Keller, A. C. Leon, et al, 'Multiple recurrences of major depressive disorder', *American Journal of Psychiatry*, 157, 2nd February 2000: 229 –233

[7] Available from the Iona Institute: http:/www.ionainstitute.ie (accessed 5th November 2015).

[8] Harold G. Koenig *Faith and Mental Health: Religious resources for Healing*. Chapter4 Religion, Psychiatric Symptoms and Disorders: 88-101 (This gives details on many studies on the relationship between depression and religion.) (Templeton Foundation Press, 2005)

Recommended resources

Depression: short animated video produced by the Royal College of Psychiatrists Public Engagement Committee in conjunction with Damn Fine Media.

Aware (helping those in Northern Ireland affected by depression): www.aware-ni.org (helpline: 08451 202961) (accessed 4th September 2015).

Depression Alliance (workshops, support and publications for those with depression): www.depressionalliance.org (accessed 4th September 2015).

Depression UK (promoting mutual support for those suffering or at risk from depression): www.depressionuk.org (accessed 4th September 2015).

Bipolar UK (supports people with a diagnosis of Bipolar Disorder and their families): www.bipolaruk.org.uk (accessed 4th September 2015).

Relate (counselling service for all kinds of relationships): www.relate.org.uk (accessed 4th September 2015).

Seasonal Affective Disorders Association (SADA) (information and help for those with Seasonal Affective Disorder): www.sada.org.uk (accessed 4th September 2015).

The Mood Gym and e-Couch (cognitive-behavioural therapy skills for preventing and coping with depression): https://moodgym.anu.edu.au/welcome (accessed 4th September 2015).

Chapter four
Spiritual help in depression

So far, I have been discussing depression in general and clinical terms. I would now like to move on to discuss how the Christian faith in particular benefits those who may suffer from depression.

As Patricia Casey's work has shown us, there is a definite connection between religious practice and mental health. Casey goes on to discuss the concept of resilience. The person who regularly engages in religious practice often has greater resilience.

What does she mean by this? One example that can help us here is to consider two cars. One car has a lot of air in its tyres and the tyres of the other are almost flat. If one drives along a bumpy road with flat tyres, every bump on the road will be felt. However, if there is plenty of air in the tyres, the bumps are experienced to a lesser degree. In other words, the air in the tyres gives greater resilience. When one goes through the stresses and pressures of life, if there is an inward resilience, then the bumps seem to be less. I think this concept of resilience is helpful in understanding the interplay between religious practice and mental health.

From a Christian perspective, I believe the Christian faith gives great benefit to those who are struggling with mental health issues. This does not mean that there is necessarily less experience of emotional pain, but it does mean that there is an undergirding reality given by the Christian faith.

Can Christians be depressed?

Although we might say that religious practice is preventive in mental health issues, it is equally true that Christians may get depressed. Reasons for this may have become clear already in this book. Some factors for depression are linked to childhood experiences which are common to all, and other problems occur as a result of loss and pain in life.

The famous preacher, Charles Spurgeon, suffered from bouts of severe depression. He had the courage to be open about his difficulties. He wrote, in *When a Preacher is Downcast*:[1]

Fits of depression come over most of us. Cheerful as we may be, we must at intervals be cast down. The strong are not always vigorous, the wise not always ready, the brave not always courageous, and the joyous not always happy.

He adds:

Knowing by most painful experience what deep depression of spirit means, being visited therewith at seasons by no means few or far between, I thought it might be consolatory to some of my brethren if I gave my thoughts thereon.

He lists several reasons why a preacher like himself might become depressed. He discusses the frailty of our general human condition, the struggles of Christian ministry and feelings of loneliness and isolation that can accompany it. He also mentions lack of exercise and recreation and failure to take regular vacations as contributory factors. He also reflects on the way God can use our feelings of weakness to keep us humble and dependent on Him.

There was once a major tragedy in his ministry. On the evening of 19th October 1856, he was preaching to a very large crowd at the Royal Surrey Gardens Music Hall. The hall itself held 12,000 people, and it was estimated that there were a further 10,000 in the gardens outside. The building was filled to capacity when, whilst Spurgeon was praying, some malicious individuals called out, 'Fire! The galleries are giving way!'[2] In the ensuing pandemonium, seven people died and 28 were admitted to hospital with severe injuries. Spurgeon had to be literally carried from the pulpit and spent several days in deep depression. Later he remarked, 'Perhaps never soul went so near the burning furnace of insanity, and yet came away unharmed.' Following this disaster, Spurgeon suffered more severely from depression, yet he also knew in his heart that his experiences helped him to minister to others even more effectively.

Christians do suffer from depression, and Spurgeon suffered more than most. His physical health was poor with chronic, painful gout, and the demands of his ministry and the music hall tragedy all took their toll. Likewise, when we experience depression, our response to it can either make us or break us. Spurgeon became stronger through what he endured. In our pain and depression, if we respond in the right way, the experience can become formative for us and can help us grow in our Christian lives.

The Bible has many examples of people who really struggled in their lives. Many of these became suicidal or even wished they had never been born. In each situation, we can see that in spite of their difficult experiences, God moved in their lives to help them. His actions in their lives are inspiring.

• The first example is the interesting story of the prophet Elijah, which we can read in 1 Kings. It was a very difficult period in the history of Israel. Ahab the king was on the throne and had married Jezebel, who was from Phoenicia. She brought with her foreign deities, which began to be worshipped in Israel, and with her came prophets of Baal and Asherah who caused the people of the land to sin. As a response to this there was no rain for three and a half years because God closed the heavens. Finally, God called Elijah to intervene again in the matters of the nation in a major showdown on Mount Carmel between the false prophets and the one true God. In this dramatic scene, God answered by fire from heaven and was seen to be the true and living God. Elijah then ordered all the prophets of Baal and Asherah to be captured and slain. Then he knew that the God who answered by fire was also the God who could send rain. The rain could come again because the false prophets had been cut off from the land. When Elijah knew the rain was on its way, he gathered his tunic around him and ran 17 miles in front of the chariot of Ahab all the way to Jezreel. By then he must have been totally exhausted – physically and mentally and spiritually, through the intensity of the conflict and physical exertion. Then Jezebel, the queen, declared that Elijah would lose his life within 24 hours. Having just faced the violent contest on Mount Carmel and experienced the hostility of the false prophets, he now ran for his life out into the desert to escape from Queen Jezebel. In this period of weakness, he collapsed under a tree and said that he wanted to die. 'I have had enough, Lord,' he said. 'Take my life, for I am no better than my ancestors' (1 Kings 19:4). God met Elijah at the point of his exhaustion and provided water and bread to sustain him. God was very gentle with this prophet and did not condemn him at all. Then Elijah went to Mount Horeb and God recommissioned him, giving him further important work to do.

Here we see an example of someone who had become physically exhausted through the tremendous stress and pressure he had been enduring. Following an intense period of exertion, Elijah became depressed and asked that he would live no longer. However, God still had wonderful plans for him.

How does this relate to depression in our lives? Physical factors can have a major part to play in depression. Also, if we totally exhaust ourselves, then we may collapse into a depressed state. It is important to understand the physical problems that may be present in depression, and sometimes if we take little sleep and do not give enough time for recreation and normal living, then we may become depressed.

- A second example of someone who really struggled in his life was Job, in the Old Testament. We know that he was an important man who was highly regarded and was one of the leaders of his city – one of the ones who used to sit with the elders at the city gate and decide weighty matters. He was also a man with a large family and many possessions. However, there came a day when, in quick succession, he lost everything. His sons and daughters lost their lives. He lost all of his possessions. All his herds of animals were taken from him. And then it tells us that his health deteriorated, and he became subject to very painful sores. We read of him down on the ground, scratching his skin with broken pottery, and bemoaning his fate. In the midst of all this, his wife turned against him and started berating him for his situation. His friends (or supposed friends) came to see him, and all of them told him again and again that he must be a very sinful man. The message they had for Job was that it was his own fault that he was in this situation. Job was confused and did not understand what had happened to him. He had lost almost everything that was important to him. In the midst of this tremendous physical, spiritual and mental pain Job was very, very downcast. Job 3:3 tells us, 'May the day of my birth perish'. In verses 20 and 21, he cried, 'Why is light given to those in misery, and life to the bitter of soul, to those who long for death that does not come, who search for it more than for hidden treasure ...' Job not only bemoaned the fact that he had been born, he also longed for death and could not find it. This was the state of someone who had been brought very low through the loss of everything, and could not understand why all this had happened to him.

This is the reality of life for some people. They lose everything that is important to them. There can be a single major loss or a series of losses in their lives. The death of a child is a very serious loss. The ending of a marital relationship can be extremely painful. The loss of all one's possessions, as happened to many in the recent economic downturn, can be very difficult to endure. In these situations people can find it hard to face the future.

However, in the middle of the most traumatic situation, Job did find light in a new way. In chapter 19 we find a glorious, triumphant shout of faith, despite the fact that his situation had not in any way materially changed. Here is his triumphant cry:

> I know that my redeemer lives,
> and that in the end he will stand on the earth.
> And after my skin has been destroyed,
> yet in my flesh I will see God.
> *Job 19:25–26*

Job became triumphant in his faith. His trial became a pathway to renewed faith in God. At the end of the story,

God restored to Job double of what he had lost, because God was gracious and giving and caring towards him.

So in these two characters, Elijah and Job, we see different factors that lead them both to the point of not wanting to carry on with life. In the case of Elijah, it is largely physical factors, and in the case of Job, it is tremendous losses that he cannot understand.

- The third example to consider is the Old Testament prophet Jeremiah. He was a prophet called to a most difficult situation. The people of Judah were about to go into captivity in Babylon. Jeremiah was given the onerous task of warning the people for the last time to turn away from their wickedness to serve the living God. His message was universally rejected by the people, by the prophets and priests and by the court and the king. No one accepted his message. He was imprisoned. He was thrown down into a pit. He was maligned by everyone. His family and the people from Anathoth where he grew up turned against him as well, and that made things extremely hard for him. During this overwhelming rejection he cries out, 'Cursed be the day I was born!' (Jeremiah 20:14).

Jeremiah really wanted to give up on life completely. He could not tolerate all the rejection and pain. His life was not an easy one. In the midst of rejection, God met him time and time again, and the depth of relationship between Jeremiah and God is inspiring for those who walk through the valley of rejection and pain.

- A fourth example of someone who went through a tremendous crisis in his life was King David. He let God down badly at one stage. He was guilty of adultery with Bathsheba, of the murder of her husband Uriah and of major deceit. During this time in his life we can see, through some of the psalms, the agony of spirit and intense depression that David experienced. David calls out:

Because of your wrath there is no health in my body;
there is no soundness in my bones because of my sin.
My guilt has overwhelmed me
like a burden too heavy to bear …
I am bowed down and brought very low;
all day long I go about mourning.
My back is filled with searing pain;
there is no health in my body.
I am feeble and utterly crushed;
I groan in anguish of heart …
even the light has gone from my eyes.
Psalm 38:3–4, 6-8, 10

David was suffering intensely, both physically and mentally. He felt cut off from God's presence. But then he turned back to God and found the reality of forgiveness:

Blessed is the one
whose transgressions are forgiven,
whose sins are covered.
Blessed is the one
whose sin the LORD does not count against them
Psalm 32:1–2

This is the account of a man who became totally broken as a result of the sin in his life. David was full of grief, melancholy and physical complaints, and it was all related to his sin. Depression can have many causes, but sometimes guilt can bring us into crushing difficulties. This was the case with King David. The way out of his predicament was to confess his sins to God and return to Him. In this way he found complete release. There are examples of this nowadays in the realm of mental health. We cannot ignore the fact that some problems may be related to real guilt. Confession and forgiveness are necessary. Another cause of depression can be our unwillingness to forgive other people. Many times we meet people whose relationships are so broken because unforgiveness is present. Giving and receiving of forgiveness can be therapeutic and healing. There is some evidence that benefits such as reduced heart rate and blood pressure can result from forgiveness.[3]

In these four biblical examples we see the effects of different situations in people's lives. All four had experiences of feeling very low and depressed. At least three of them were suicidal. All four felt cut off from God at times. In each case, God dealt with them differently. Elijah, who was physically exhausted, was given food and drink. Job found new faith in his toil and difficulty. Jeremiah was totally rejected by everyone, but the relationship he had with God was very close and personal, and this sustained him. In David's situation, when he confessed his sin and returned to the Lord, God graciously forgave and restored him.

In our lives, even when we go through periods of severe depression, God is with us. The wonderful promise of Jesus is still the same, 'And surely I am with you always, to the very end of the age' (Matthew 28:20).

Around two years ago, I gave a talk on depression in the south of Ireland. It was a long journey and not many were present. After I had given the first talk on the medical and psychiatric aspects of depression, I was approached by a lady during the interval before the second talk. She looked extremely depressed and, as I usually do, I asked her whether she would consider booking an appointment with a local family doctor. Then, in the second part, I emphasised how Christ can come into our lives and make a real difference. From the front I led a prayer of confession of our sins and receiving Christ into our lives. This lady prayed to receive Christ into her life. At the end I hardly recognised her, because her face was beaming with new joy. In her case, the change was quite dramatic. It does not always happen this way!

Summary of chapters three and four

- Depression can be a serious illness with a range of causes.

- It can have marked effects on our health and well-being.

- It may need rapid treatment, and an understanding of the various treatments can be helpful.

- Those who engage in religious practice tend to have less depression.

- Religious practice can result in increased resilience.

- Christians can battle with depression, but can come out of it stronger than before.

---

[1] Charles Spurgeon, *When a Preacher is Downcast*, www.haven.today.org/spurgeon-on-depression-gd-434.html (accessed 10th September 2015).

[2] Dr Darrel W. Amundsen, 'The Anguish and Agonies of Charles Spurgeon', *Christianity Today*: www.ctlibrary.com (accessed 3rd September 2015).

[3] K. A. Lawler, J.W. Younger, R. L. Piferi et al, 'A change of heart: Cardiovascular correlates of forgiveness in response to interpersonal conflict'. *Journal of Behavioural Medicine* 26:373-393 (2003).

Chapter five
The person who is suicidal

I have been involved recently in leading training sessions for Street Pastors. This is an excellent organisation, run by volunteers who go out onto the streets late at night in all kinds of weather to give practical support to those whom they meet. I give training on how they can help people who have mental health issues. I usually do this by providing some short stories of people they might meet. All of these stories are purposely fictitious and are not intended to relate to any one individual.

Here is a case history that I use in training.

We will call this 45-year-old man Tommy. He seems to be walking quite aimlessly and you get talking to him. He has had a few drinks but can still tell you about his problems. Apart from the alcohol on his breath, he looks unkempt and has not shaved recently. He was working as a long-distance lorry driver for many years, but he lost his job a few months back, and although he has been trying, he cannot find another one. He married his childhood sweetheart, Elaine, at the age of 21, but his wife left him a couple of years ago for another man, taking their two children with her. He has not seen any of them for some time. He admits to drinking, mainly at weekends as he feels bored. He has run up some debts on his credit cards and does not know how he will pay them off. As a casual remark he asks if you know anyone who would like to buy his dog, a yellow Labrador. He believes in God but cannot understand how God could allow all these bad things to happen in his life. He lives alone and has few friends and has not been eating so well recently.

In a training setting I would ask, 'What key question would you ask Tommy?', 'What other questions would you like to ask?', 'What help would you offer Tommy?'

These questions often promote quite a degree of interaction and discussion in small groups around coffee tables.

I want someone to ask Tommy the key question, 'Are you all right?' or, 'Are you OK?' or, 'How are you feeling?' This allows the person freedom to discuss and reveal their current feelings and problems. As Tommy begins to talk about his problems, one can then ask further questions. Another very important question in this situation is to ask why he wants to sell his dog. The thought behind this question is to work out why he is making this decision at this point in his life. The answer is that he may be trying to sort out his affairs, and he may actually be suicidal.

Once one has asked the question about whether he is all right, it is helpful to gently ask further key leading questions. If he admits to feeling rather low, one can ask questions such as, 'How low are you feeling?', 'Have you been feeling more down recently?', 'Are you feeling very low and down?', 'How does the future seem? Is life still worth living?', 'Have you ever had thoughts of self-harm?', 'Have you had any suicidal thoughts?', 'Have you made any suicidal plans?' This needs to be done in a sensitive and caring way after a degree of rapport has been established with Tommy. If one asks the questions too early in the interview, then the responses may not be accurate. He may try to hide what is going on, as he may perceive that the questions have been too abrupt. Initially he might be unwilling to answer, whilst later on, once rapport has been established, he might be much more ready to disclose his inner thoughts. If somebody is truly suicidal, then it is imperative to find help.

You gently ask Tommy a few more questions, and he begins to open up.

'How are you, Tommy? How are you feeling? Are you OK?'

Tommy starts hesitatingly. He says that in the last month things have been really bad. He struggles to get out of bed in the morning and often does not get up till midday.

'I am not eating much,' he says. 'I might open a tin of baked beans. I can't be bothered to cook.'

He tells you that he used to go to the Horse and Hounds some nights for a couple of beers, but he can't afford to do that any more.

'I'm in debt,' he adds. 'Over £3,000 on my credit card, and I don't know how I will pay it off.'

'Can't be bothered to do anything,' he mutters.

'I often toss and turn all night. In the early mornings, that's when it's worst,' he says.

'What's the point?' he asks. 'I have no friends. Since I lost my job, my workmates don't keep in touch. Every day seems the same. I have nothing really to live for. I keep asking myself why Elaine moved out. I thought my wife and I were getting on fine, and then one day there was this note: "Sorry, Tommy, it's no good; I've found someone else. I am picking up Phelim and Bridget from school and I may not see you for a while." I haven't heard from her since, and that's two years ago. I haven't seen Phelim and Bridget for the past year. I know I was drinking more than I should, but she shouldn't have left me just like that.'

Tommy is obviously very bitter. And now he states, 'I don't care whether I live or die.'

You ask him gently about the future. 'Haven't got any future,' he declares.

'Tell me about the Labrador,' you ask, changing the subject.

'Lovely dog, Goldie,' he says, with tears welling up in his eyes, 'but I can't afford to feed her, and I want her to get a good home. I can't manage her any longer.'

'But why are you selling her now?' you gently ask. Tommy looks at the ground and is silent.

'Can't cope any longer,' he says. 'I'm just on the way to the river. There's a bridge there. I just want to finish everything. There's just so much pain. I can't take any more.'

By now you are very concerned, and are wondering what to do next. You ask him if he would be willing to come and talk to the team leader, but he says, 'No, I've got to go.'

Just then you see a couple of policemen walking by. You call them over. You blurt out in desperation, 'This guy, Tommy, says he is on the way to the river to jump off the bridge. Can you help me, please?'

The policemen begin talking to Tommy and are able to persuade him after a while to come with them to the local hospital. You ask Tommy if he would like you to come too and he agrees.

Depending on the situation, the initial help might be from a friendly local police officer (if one is on the street, with little other resource available and Tommy is truly suicidal) or it might be from the local casualty department, or it might be from a health professional, depending on the gravity of the situation.

The Golden Gate Bridge in San Francisco has been the place where many people have died by suicide. Around

1,500 have jumped off the bridge. There have only been about 30 survivors, giving a figure of one in 50 who have survived the jump. Recently the authorities in the area have been in the process of putting up nets to prevent further casualties. On many other bridges, barriers have been built around them. In the case of the Golden Gate Bridge, this would not be effective as high winds might destroy or distort the barriers, making them ineffective. The idea of nets in this particular situation, although costing in the region of $76 million, seems a better solution.

One person who jumped from the bridge was a man called Kevin Hines. His story is freely available online and recently appeared in an issue of the journal *Advances in Psychiatric Treatment* under the title of 'Hey, kid, are you OK?'

The account of his story is illuminating.[1]

Initially at school he was doing very well and was involved in many activities. He was an athlete, involved in debating and student government, with an active social life and good family support. At the age of 17, however, he was diagnosed as suffering from bipolar affective disorder. In this condition there are periods of intense depression followed by periods of hyperactivity and mania or a lesser degree of mania referred to as hypomania. In his case the mood swings were quite severe, and he also began to hear voices that were talking to him, and he found the experience very distressing. He struggled to follow treatment plans and began to abuse alcohol.

He began to withdraw from activities and became extremely depressed. He felt alone and hopeless, to the point of becoming suicidal. By September 2000 he could feel only intense emotional pain. One night he wrote seven or eight separate suicide notes, finally settling on one of these. His father had become so concerned about him that he wanted to take him into work with him the following day to ensure his safety. However, his father discussed the matter with the doctor, who told him that he did not need to be that concerned. As it turned out, his father's concern was not misplaced. On that morning, Kevin Hines decided to go to the Golden Gate Bridge by bus. On the way, the bus conductor told him quite abruptly to get off the bus since Kevin was obviously delaying getting off and was very tearful.

Kevin then walked up and down on the Golden Gate Bridge for around 40 minutes, with tears streaming down his face. He had decided if anyone asked him what his problem was, he would tell them the whole story and probably not jump. No one stopped him to ask whether he was OK. The only person who stopped him was a beautiful girl, and her request was that he might take her photograph, which he duly did.

He decided to climb up, and then he jumped off the bridge. Instantly he realised he had made a terrible mistake. During the seven to eight seconds it took to reach the water, he prayed fervently that God would actually save his life.

On hitting the water something amazing happened. A sea lion kept nosing him to the surface until the Coast Guard boat arrived. (Apparently this is not unknown animal behaviour.) He was seriously injured and spent two weeks in intensive medical care and then several months in psychiatric care before being released.

Since that time, although he has had further bouts of illness, he has been generally well. He now goes around the world telling people about the importance of having structure in their lives, as one way that can help mental health problems.

Kevin's story illustrates something quite important. The moment his feet left the bridge he knew instantly that he did not actually want to die. Many people with suicidal thoughts do not actually want to die; it is just that they are often coping with intense emotional pain, and in this pain, suicide seems the only way out.

What is suicide?

The answer to this might seem quite obvious. However, one definition that I think is helpful is this: 'Suicide is a multi-dimensional malaise in a needful individual, who defines an issue for which the suicide is perceived as the best solution.'[2]

This definition implies that there are often several interrelated reasons why a person may finally decide to end their life by suicide. The person is needy, and cannot cope with the many problems that they are facing at that particular point in time. There is intense emotional pain that cannot be contained. To this person, at this time, suicide seems the only solution. Suicide is, as has been expressed by American media personality Phil Donahue, 'a permanent solution to a temporary problem'.[3]

Intense emotional pain will not last forever. Even Tommy's emotional pain, as described in the training scenario above, is temporary. It is very difficult to contain or continue in a state of intense emotional pain (so great as might lead to suicide) for long periods of time. Feelings have limits, and the powerful suicidal feelings are often quite short-lived. However, in the midst of this intense emotional pain, a person feels that they cannot cope, and suicide seems the only way out.

The suicide rate worldwide is high. The World Health Organization recorded a 60 per cent increase in the rate of death by suicide over a 45-year period up to 2002.[4] There are more than 800,000 suicides worldwide each year.[5] In the UK in 2013 there were 6,233 deaths by suicide in those over the age of 15, compared with 1,713 from road traffic accidents.[6] The rate of suicide in men is considerably higher than it is in women. British men are now around three times as likely to die by suicide as women. It is now the single biggest cause of death in men aged 20 to 49 in England and Wales. On an average day in the United Kingdom, 12 men take their lives. In Ireland the suicide rate is around 500 per year. In Northern Ireland the rate has increased by almost 100 per cent in the last 15 years. The rate in Northern Ireland was the highest in the UK in 2012.[7]

Many will know of 'The Troubles' that affected the people of Northern Ireland between 1968 and 1998. During this period of civil unrest, around 3,600 people lost their lives. I used to see people in my clinic who had been traumatised by the situations which they had to deal with during The Troubles. I saw prison officers, policemen and firefighters who had been involved in dealing with bombs, deaths and their aftermath, who still struggled to live normally because their lives had been deeply traumatised, and they endured repeated reliving of their terrible experiences.

However, statistically between 1998 and 2012, there were almost 3,300 suicides. In 14 years, the number of suicides has almost equalled the number of killings over what was almost a 30-year period.[8]

The relationship between suicidal thoughts, suicidal attempts, suicidal plans and actual completed suicide

Professor Patricia Casey looked at how commonly suicidal thoughts were found in various countries. In five countries in the European Union, the presence of suicidal ideas in the population ranged from one per cent to 19 per cent.[9] In another study in 17 countries, of those who had suicidal thoughts, 29 per cent made a suicidal attempt, usually within a year of onset of the thoughts. However, of those who had a definite suicidal plan, 56 per cent made an attempt. Of those without a plan, only 15 per cent made an attempt.[10] These figures show that it is very important to determine whether a person has an actual suicidal plan. If a plan is present, there is a much greater likelihood of a suicide attempt. Of those who make a suicidal attempt, 85 to 90 per cent never actually complete the suicide.

There has been a very interesting study of people who had been on the Golden Gate Bridge and were preparing to jump, but a highway patrol was able to reach them just before they did so. Psychologist Richard Seiden reports that of 515 people who were stopped on the point of making a suicidal attempt, 90 per cent of them were still alive 25 years later, or had died by natural causes.[11] These figures show that if one is able to intervene at the point of a person's making a suicidal attempt, this can preserve lives.

What are some of the risk factors for suicide?

There are several factors in a person's history that can be important pointers. Has this person self-harmed? Is there mental illness in the family? Has anyone in the family died by suicide? In Tommy's case, his wife and family had left him two years previously. When he was finally assessed in the Accident and Emergency department, his records showed that he had taken a lot of tablets the previous year, but someone had called at the house unexpectedly and had managed to get him to hospital. What age is the person? In Northern Ireland, middle-aged men who have survived The Troubles are at increased risk.

Then there are certain aspects of an individual's life that may be rapidly changing. Suicidal ideas tend to vary in their severity over time. Often there may be a sense of hopelessness. If hopelessness is present, it can be a worrying feature, and this was the case with Tommy. He really could see no future for himself. His current debts and financial problems, loneliness and isolation were pushing him towards the brink. A person may also be under considerable psychological stress.

Another factor to consider is whether the person has access to a method of suicide. Certain preventative measures have been carried out on a large scale, which have actually helped reduce the suicide rate by particular means. For example, in Bristol, UK, there is a famous bridge called the Clifton Suspension Bridge. Following many suicides, barriers were erected and the suicide rate from this bridge has dropped by 50 per cent. However, what is interesting is that those who go to the bridge wanting to die by suicide, and then find that they cannot, because of the barriers, rarely go to another bridge to complete the suicide. Having been foiled in their attempt in one situation, the intensity of their suicidal thoughts diminishes, and they do not actually complete the suicide.[12] This shows that barriers on bridges can save lives.

Also, reducing the toxicity in car exhausts by catalytic converters and detoxifying gas can save lives. The provision of blister packs and limiting the amount of paracetamol a person can purchase, can prevent people from overdosing, again saving lives. So these different measures which have been carried out on a large scale can be preventative.

Another factor to consider in suicide risk is the quality of contact with the psychiatric service. This is very important.

Tommy (the man with the Labrador) is seen in the local Accident and Emergency department. By this stage he has calmed down a bit. He sits with his head held in his hands, looking at the floor. He doesn't say much but seems pleased that you have stayed with him.

After rather a long wait, the doctor asks him to come in, and asks if you would mind waiting outside. Tommy is with the doctor for quite a while. Tommy tells you about it afterwards. 'She was very calm and seemed to understand everything I was going through,' he says. 'She asked a lot of questions, and I told her everything that was going on. She asked me about one incident where I had taken tablets before. I told her that when I had taken the tablets, I had seen a psychiatrist on the ward a couple of days later, and he had given me some pills and had said I was depressed, but I didn't take the pills, and I didn't go back for another appointment.'

Follow-up of someone who has self-harmed is very important, but can be difficult to arrange. Once started on antidepressants, it is important to continue to take them regularly over a period of time to obtain benefit.

What is the risk of suicide if a person has a pre-existing mental illness?

Let us look at risks of suicide in those who have mental health conditions. There are certain high-risk groups. Those who have a history of psychiatric illness are at risk. People with psychiatric problems may have had difficulty adhering to treatment plans. If there have been previous self-harm or suicide attempts, this may cause concern. If they have been recently discharged from a psychiatric hospital or institution, the risk is greater. If there is the presence of alcohol or drug misuse, again this is a worrying feature. In Tommy's case, the alcohol he had taken and the previous self-harm and depression placed him at increased risk.

Of those with severe depression, schizophrenia or alcohol dependence, around six to seven per cent will eventually kill themselves. Suicide is common in those with severe personality disorder and drug misuse. Personality disorder has been defined as 'An enduring pattern of inner experience and behaviour that deviates markedly from the expectations of the individual's culture'.[13] Those with epilepsy and poor physical health are similarly at increased risk.

Of those who die by suicide it has been estimated that 90 per cent have some kind of psychiatric disorder.[14] It is also true that doctors find it difficult to fully assess suicidal risk. This, of course, depends on what information is given by the patient. Many of us have been surprised by those who take their own lives. Often they have failed to reveal their true thoughts and intentions. However, if the quality of contact with psychiatric services is seen as positive, then the person is much more likely to reveal the content of their thoughts, and lives can be saved.

What is the connection between social situations and the risk of suicide?

The recent economic downturn has been associated with an increase in the suicide rate over the last few years in many Western countries. The rate is higher in areas with high unemployment and poverty. For two years I lived in West Belfast, where there is a very high suicide rate. Here there is a high unemployment rate, marked social deprivation, and many similar problems. The rate of suicide is higher where there is social fragmentation, and this is an alarming feature of modern society. With Tommy, the loss of his wife and family had led to a very isolated and lonely existence. In today's culture many more people now live by themselves. In those who do live alone, and have sustained recent severe loss in their lives, the suicide risk is higher. It is also higher in those who face criminal charges.

It is important that the media and television do not glamourise or give too much detail regarding suicides. There were many 'copycat' suicides following the death of Marilyn Monroe, for example. This is sometimes referred to as the 'Werther Effect'. (Goethe's novel *The Sorrows of Young Werther* was widely read in Europe around 200 years ago. The suicide of the hero was widely imitated, leading to the banning of the book in some countries.) The media, in general, is now much more responsive and responsible in the way that it describes suicide, and this is helpful.

Other social situations may be related to suicide. There is an increased rate amongst widowers, widows and the divorced. The rate is lower in those who are married. It is high amongst those who are unemployed, amongst prisoners and those on remand. There is variation in the suicide rate amongst different social classes. The suicide rate is highest in the lowest social class, and this is followed by the top social class. (The structure of society in the UK is divided into social classes on the basis of wealth, occupation and education.) Certain professions are at risk of suicide. The risk is high in vets, pharmacists, doctors, farmers, students and sailors.

What are 'red flag' signs of possible impending suicide?

(In much of this following discussion on suicide, I am heavily indebted to two excellent papers by Alys Cole-King and others which were published in *Advances in Psychiatric Treatment* (now *BJPsych Advances*) in July 2013).[15]

There are certain situations which should cause alarm if they are present. These 'red flag' situations should cause us to stop and consider carefully whether someone might indeed be at high risk of suicide.

The presence of a well-formed suicide plan and preparations is very worrying. If hopelessness is present and the person can only see a short future for themselves, this raises the level of concern. Tommy had decided to end everything, had no hope left, and was heading to the nearest bridge over the river. A person's mental experiences may make them vulnerable. Sometimes people with mental illness may have strange experiences which are very real to them. They may have thoughts of persecution, where they are convinced that others want to harm them in some way. They may also experience voices talking to them. If these voices command the person to carry out certain actions, and the person feels that they have to obey these commands, this can be very worrying, particularly if the voices tell the person to self-harm, or harm others.

Some people, like Tommy, feel trapped by various stresses and problems in their lives and cannot see a way out. Those with pain and chronic medical conditions are at risk. I found that I needed to assess, very carefully, the elderly who were in pain and feeling depressed, and I used to see this combination quite frequently. The risk in these people is higher than it would be if they did not have the pain. Also, the risk is higher in those recently diagnosed with medical conditions such as cancer, or similar serious illness, or who have experienced a loss of function, such as the loss of eyesight or the loss of ability to walk.

Those who have a lack of social support, like Tommy, or have no one to confide in, or have been recently bereaved, are more vulnerable. I can recall many people who have been in hospital with severe depression and suicidal thoughts, who had recently lost someone very important to them. Relationships are very significant. If there is major instability in a relationship, this can increase the risk.

If there is significant concern about a risk of suicide, then developing a safety plan is important. The following box offers some good advice.

Helping a person to stay safe

1. If there is an immediate suicide risk, get help straight away. Make sure someone stays with the person and remove access to means of suicide. Arrange urgent medical assessment.

2. If the person says that they will not harm themselves, can they be believed?

3. Following assessment a safety plan might be devised. This would include ways of dealing with suicidal thoughts.

4. They should be encouraged to keep with them a list of contact details of supportive friends and relatives.

5. Ensure they have contact details for emergency professional and voluntary support.

6. There should be a strategy in place of what to do if suicidal thoughts become stronger or more persistent.

7. The 'Feeling on the Edge' booklet can be very helpful: http://www.rcpsych.ac.uk/mentalhealthinfo/proble ms/feelingon theedge.aspx (accessed 1st October 2015).

How can we approach those who are at risk of suicide?

Recently in psychiatric literature, there has been marked interest in what we might call a compassionate approach to suicide prevention. This emphasises the importance of understanding and compassion. It discusses the need to enquire about suicidal thoughts in a sensitive manner. There is always the need to understand the risks of suicide, and conducting a proper assessment is vital. However, this compassionate approach emphasises that we need to try to increase hopefulness, resilience, and reasons for living. If we are able to do this, then we can reduce the suicide risk.

Compassion emphasises two qualities. The first is identification with the person who is feeling suicidal; the second is the commitment to do something about it. It has been shown that if people with suicidal thoughts find people friendly and willing to help, then suicidal thoughts are reduced. The doctor demonstrated this compassionate approach in her interaction with Tommy. He said that she was very understanding, and he felt that he could tell her all his problems.

Six essential qualities of compassion[16]

- Firstly, there needs to be the motivation to help the person in need.

- Secondly, there needs to be sensitivity to the person and their need.

- Thirdly, there is the need to be non-judgemental; in other words, having the capacity of not passing judgement on what one might be told.

- Fourthly, sympathy is important. This is an ability to feel for the person.

- Fifthly, the person needs to find the ability to continue to listen and understand, despite feeling distressed by the situation.

- Lastly, accurate empathy is also required. This goes beyond sympathy. It actually tries to understand the way the person is feeling in their particular situation.

These six qualities are important and essential qualities of compassion.

How can hope and 'connectedness' be improved?

If people feel well supported socially, and are connected well to others, then these factors can be protective against suicidal behaviour. On the other hand, loneliness and social isolation are often related to depression and suicidal behaviour.

The doctor wanted to make one or two suggestions to Tommy. However, because he had been so set on suicide and was still somewhat ambivalent and also clearly suffering from severe depression, she was able to persuade him to stay in hospital for a short while until he was feeling better and more able to cope with life.

Helping to increase 'connectedness' can be done by various means. A recent study showed that those who received caring letters by post following treatment in hospital for self-harm had a reduced repetition rate of 50 per cent. [17] Making telephone contact with a person a month after discharge following a self-poisoning episode showed benefit in terms of reduced repetition of attempted suicide. [18]

Later, you ask Tommy if he had received any caring letters or phone calls following his taking the tablets on the previous occasion. 'No, not from anyone,' he said. You wonder if it might have helped him if someone had been in touch in a caring way.

One concept worth considering is referred to as 'The Bank of Hope'. [19] The idea here is to try to put more hope in the 'bank' of the person who might currently be feeling hopeless. In doing this, the aim is to try to encourage people to believe that their suicidal thoughts and feelings will often be short-lived. If they can look beyond their suicidal thoughts, this can help them. Often a person's desire is to feel better, not actually to end their life. It can be very helpful to try to persuade people to look beyond their immediate situations and to focus on solutions rather than on the current problems.

On the ward, Tommy likes the nursing staff, and every day a rather shy nurse called Gemma comes to talk to him. He finds it easy to open up to her. Betty, the social worker, spends some time with him, helping him to find a clear strategy to manage his debts, and also has some ideas about future employment. He is very pleased to see you when you call, and is glad that you have been able to get Goldie the Labrador well looked after. The psychiatrist has seen him, and after a lengthy discussion has helped him look beyond the crisis, and Tommy has agreed to start an antidepressant. Even Eddie, his half-brother from Scotland, has looked in and Tommy really enjoyed seeing him for the first time in a year. Eddie has offered to have Tommy come and stay with him for a while, and he is thinking about this.

How can we help people to look beyond the immediate crisis?

One question that can be asked is this: 'If you were to go to bed tonight and a miracle happened and all these suicidal thoughts went, what would be the first thing that you would notice in the morning?' The purpose of this type of question is to try to get people to look beyond the immediate situation, and to look at a possible scenario where their suicidal thoughts may have actually gone.

A second question which can be helpful is to ask the person, 'How did you cope with previous difficult and distressing situations?' Or a similar question might be to ask, 'When you look back on this testing period in your life, what do you think will have been the main thing that got you through it?'

How can we help a person develop resilience in their life?

As well as helping somebody to look beyond the immediate crisis, it can be important to try to help the person develop resilience. Resilience is the ability to cope with crises and difficulties in a better way. There are certain ways in which one might aim to increase resilience. As we have discussed, 'connectedness' is very important. Eddie, Tommy's half-brother, is helping him to feel less isolated. Aiming to increase 'connectedness' by various activities can be very useful. For example, we might encourage people to maintain links with family and friends. We might help motivate someone to join in group activities. In my clinic I used to suggest to older people that they might become more socially involved. Having pets or encouraging hobbies and sports can be very valuable. Being involved with music or exercise – particularly group exercise – can be helpful. People can be encouraged to distract themselves when suicidal thoughts are intense by learning to switch away from these thoughts. This can be by moving to some definite different activity such as reading, or watching television, or focusing on something else entirely as a means of alleviating the intense emotional pain which they are going through.

Learning to be kind to oneself is important. Many people feel very driven by their situations, but encouraging them or helping them to take a break can be useful. Another way of helping people might be to encourage them to give to others in some way. A very good short documentary has been recently produced, entitled *U Can Cope*. [20] It recounts how three people overcame strong suicidal tendencies. One person explains how he began to help people with Alzheimer's disease, and he found that as he cared for others, this really helped him.

We can encourage people to keep a list of people and things that they love, on paper, or on a mobile phone, to be referred to in an emergency. They can keep a list of the contact details of those who care for them and those whom they trust, and again this list could be vital in a crisis.

One can emphasise that thousands of people feel overwhelmed every day but find ways to get through these intense feelings. We can encourage the person that, like these people, there may be a way through the immediate difficulties, and by working together this way may be found. Emphasising that the intensity of emotional experience is likely to be short-lived and that they can come through the other side is valuable. Stating that a person only has to live one day at a time can be an important message. The current distress may be a pointer to the need to change something in life, although it is usually unwise to make major changes when in crisis.

The qualities of compassion and care are very important. Seeking to help people over the initial crisis by encouraging them to focus on how they will feel after the crisis has passed is useful.

There are resources in the community which can help somebody who is suicidal. For example, Samaritans are very helpful. In the North of Ireland, Lifeline is a very useful resource. The Royal College of Psychiatrists have several booklets that are freely available to download. An organisation called Aware Defeat Depression have a helpline.

In the *U Can Cope* film there are three key messages:

- Firstly, anyone can experience suicidal thoughts.

- Secondly, there is always hope.

- Thirdly, there is always help.

The ASIST (Applied Suicide Intervention Skills Training)[21] course is also helpful in training people to recognise and help those who may be suicidal. In Northern Ireland, this course is a two-day skills-building workshop which prepares ordinary people to provide suicide first-aid interventions. Similar organisations are present in other countries.

As previously mentioned, practising a religion can help build resilience in a person's life. The work of Patricia Casey in her article entitled 'The psychosocial benefits of religious practice' emphasises that those who regularly practise their religious faith have a decreased risk of suicide.

---

[1] Kevin Hines, Alys Cole-King and Mel Blaustein, 'Hey kid, are you OK? A story of suicide survived', *Advances in Psychiatric Treatment*, 19:292–294 (2013).

[2] R. W. Maris, A. L. Berman, J. T. Maltsberger et al, 'Overview of the study of suicide assessment and prediction', in *Assessment and Prediction of Suicide*, eds R. W. Maris, A. L. Berman, J. T. Maltsberger, et al (New York, Guilford Press, 1992), pp. 3–22.

[3] Phil Donahue – American media personality, NBC TV, 23rd May 1984.

[4] World Health Organisation, 'Multisite Intervention Study on Suicidal Behaviours (SUPRE-MISS)', Department of Mental Health and Substance Dependence, WHO (2002).

[5] WHO suicide data: www.who.int/mental_health/prevention/suicide/suicideprevent/en/ (accessed 4th September 2015)

[6] 'Suicides in the United Kingdom 2013 Registrations', *ONS Statistical Bulletin* www.ons.gov.uk/ons/dcp171778_395145.pdf (accessed 04/09/2015).

[7] 'Reported road casualties in Great Britain: main results (2013)', Gov UK www.gov.uk/... reported-road-casualties-in-great-britain-main-results (accessed 4th September 2015).

[8] Kathryn Torney, 'Suicide kills as many as the Troubles – Investigation and Analysis', 10th February 2014: www.thedetail.tv/articles/suicide-kills-as-many-as-the-troubles (accessed 4th September 2015).

[9] P. Casey, G. Dunn, B. D. Kelly et al, 'The prevalence of suicidal ideation in the general population: results from the Outcome of Depression International Network (ODIN) study', *Social Psychiatry and Psychiatric Epidemiology*, 43:299–304 (2008).

[10] M. K. Nock, G. Borges, E. J. Bromet et al, 'Cross-national prevalence and risk factors for suicidal ideation, plans and attempts', *British Journal of Psychiatry*, 192:98–105 (2008).

[11] R. H. Seiden, 'Where are they now? A follow-up study of suicide attempters from the Golden Gate Bridge', *Journal of Suicide and Life Threatening Behaviour* 8:203–16 (1978).

[12] O. Bennewith, N. Nowers, D. Gunnell, 'Effect of barriers on the Clifton Suspension Bridge, England, on local patterns of suicide: implications for prevention', *British Journal of Psychiatry*, 90:266–267 (2007).

[13] American Psychiatric Association, Washington, DC: Diagnostic and Statistical Manual of Mental Disorders, 4th edn, 1994.

[14] J. T. O. Cavanagh, A. J. Carson, M. Sharpe et al, 'Psychological autopsy studies of suicide: a systematic review' *Psychological Medicine*, 33:395–405 (2003).

[15] Alys Cole-King, Gill Green, Linda Gask, Kevin Hines and Stephen Platt, 'Suicide mitigation: a compassionate approach to suicide prevention', *Advances in Psychiatric Treatment*, 19:276–

283 (July 2013). Alys Cole-King, Victoria Parker, Helen Williams and Stephen Platt, 'Suicide prevention: are we doing enough?' *Advances in Psychiatric Treatment*, 19:284–291 (2013).

[16] P. Gilbert, C. Irons, 'Focused therapies and compassionate mind training for shame and self-attacking', in P. Gilbert (ed.), *Compassion, Conceptualisations, Research and Use in Psychotherapy* (New York, Routledge, 2005), pp. 263–325.

[17] G. L. Carter, K. Clover, I. M. Whyte et al, 'Postcards from the Edge: 24 month outcomes of a randomised controlled trial for hospital treated self-poisoning', *British Journal of Psychiatry*, 191:548–553 (2007).

[18] G. Valva, F. Ducrocq, P. Meyer, et al, 'Effect of telephone contact on further suicide attempts in patients discharged from an emergency department: randomised controlled study', *BMJ*, 332:1241–6 (2006).

[19] Cole-King et al, 'Suicide mitigation: a compassionate approach to suicide prevention'.

[20] *U Can Cope film* released 10/09/2012. www.connectingwithpeople.org/ucancope (accessed 4th September 2015).

[21] ASIST from www.livingworks.net (accessed 5th September 2015).

Recommended resources

Samaritans (helpline: 08457 909090) (round-the-clock support for whatever is getting to you): www.samaritans.org (accessed 4th September 2015).

International Association for Suicide Prevention (aiming to prevent suicidal behaviour, reduce its effects and provide a forum for professional and non-professional involvement): www.iasp.info/index.php (accessed 4th September 2015).

Chapter six
Spiritual help for the suicidal person

What about the Christian who is trying to cope with suicidal thoughts? What help is there in the Christian faith for those who are struggling in this way?

One person who suffered incredible loss in his life was the missionary pioneer Adoniram Judson. In 1813 he went to Burma. On the way there his wife, Nancy, had a stillbirth and the next child, Roger, died of 'Tropical Fever'. It was six years before Judson baptised his first convert. Then in 1824 war broke out between Great Britain and Burma, and Judson was incarcerated. The conditions were atrocious. At night his ankles, bound with fetters, were hoisted up on a pole towards the ceiling so only his head and shoulders rested on the ground. The cell was infested with vermin. He was not allowed to sleep. From time to time, people were taken from the cells and executed, and no one knew who would be next. Finally, after several months, he was taken from his cell and then force-marched for a long distance to the north of the country, on bleeding and bruised feet. Several of his companions died on the way.

Each step was agony. At one point they crossed a high bridge over a deep gorge, and Judson was very tempted to end everything and go over the edge. He resisted this temptation, but life remained very difficult and he was imprisoned once again.

After the war, Judson was employed as a go-between, since he knew both English and Burmese. This meant separation from Nancy and their young daughter, Maria. Judson was away for a long time, and during this time both Nancy and Maria died. Judson could not forgive himself for not being with his wife when she needed him most. He sought to bury himself in his work of Bible translation and evangelism. He worked extremely hard over the next two years as a way of trying to deal with the tremendous sorrow he felt. However, hard work will never assuage the pangs of grief. Finally he could work no longer, and gradually his input began to decrease. He withdrew from his fellow workers. He went into the jungle, where he built a simple hut and lived completely alone. Finally, he dug a grave for himself and each day walked around the open grave with his mind full of thoughts of death. In his heart he knew that God was still there, but he had lost all sense of God's presence.

However, his Christian friends loved him and prayed for him earnestly. Gradually Judson emerged from his deep depression as a different man. Despite his most difficult experiences, there was a solid foundation to his faith. Although prior to this he had gone around preaching and had seen just a few people come to the faith, now when he preached thousands came to Christ. Through the deep depression, which extended to strong thoughts of death around an open grave, God had done a wonderful work of transformation in his life. Now he was a changed man, and the power of God in the Holy Spirit was mightily present with him.

This experience of Judson can teach us that Christians can indeed suffer depression, since they suffer the loss and pain common to humanity.

In my own life, whilst living in Cyprus, I had a very difficult experience. I was leading a church, but there were many problems and I was not sure I could continue to lead. One morning, I woke up suddenly with a Bible reference strongly in my mind. It was Matthew 7:25. I told Ros, my wife, and we looked up the verse together. It reads like this:

> The rain came down, the streams rose, and the winds blew and beat against that house; yet it did not fall, because it had its foundation on the rock.
> *Matthew 7:25*

My wife thought for a moment and then said to me, 'Steve, I believe God is saying something. Things are very difficult, and they will get worse this week. But God is telling you not to worry because He is with you, and your life is built on the rock.' Three days later, the situation I had feared really exploded. In the end, I spent days by myself in tears. I felt it better to resign from my position as leader of the church, and it was a very sad time for my wife and myself. (Although very low at times, I did not get to the very low ebb that Judson experienced.) God, however, was still with us. A year later He led us to a different city where we started afresh, and today, the church He helped us to start there is still going strongly and has expanded to several other places. When our lives are founded on the rock, He will bring fulfilment and blessing, despite the trials we may pass through.

When we experience depression, our response to it may either make us or break us. Judson emerged a different man following his experiences. In our pain and depression, if we adapt in the right way, the experience can become formative for us and can help us grow in our Christian lives.

How can we help people build resilience in their lives?

The above stories illustrate how the Christian faith helps us to be resilient when we face various trials. In the case of Judson, the support of his friends proved crucial. Building hope and resilience is very important. There are several ways of doing this. We may help someone to engage socially. Isolation and loneliness are often overwhelming problems. We may be able to help someone take an extra interest in helping others, such as the young man mentioned in the *U Can Cope* documentary, who helped those with Alzheimer's disease. Advice regarding developing a regular lifestyle and helping people find structure in their lives can be vital.

Relationships in life are extremely important. Many people may lack the motivation or the personal skills to repair these when they have fallen apart. Advising and, if necessary, assisting people to repair fractured relationships can be life-changing. Offering and receiving forgiveness can be necessary in restoring brokenness and increasing connectedness. Christ talks a lot about the importance of forgiveness. These are His words:

> For, if you forgive other people when they sin against you, your heavenly Father will also forgive you. But if you do not forgive others their sins, your Father will not forgive your sins.
> *Matthew 6:14–15*

How does Christ show us what compassion really means?

We have observed that demonstrating compassion is an important part of healthcare. This expression of compassion can be seen in the assessment process, but also in the sending of letters (or through phone calls) to those who have attended hospital following an episode of self-harm. Finding ways of building hope, and looking beyond the crisis to the future, have also been seen to be effective and helpful for the person who is experiencing suicidal thoughts.

The definition we have used of compassion implies sensitivity to distress and doing something about the problem. We find this compassion supremely demonstrated in the life of Christ. 'When he saw the crowds, he had compassion on them, because they were harassed and helpless, like sheep without a shepherd' (Matthew 9:36). Jesus sees into the heart of a person. He sees individuals who are harassed and helpless and torn and broken down. He sees each one of the crowd as an individual with struggles, pain and brokenness.

When Jesus saw individuals and their tremendous needs, He appointed His disciples to go and do the work that He was doing. His work of healing and blessing people was then multiplied. On another occasion, the crowds had been with Him for a long time:

> When Jesus landed and saw a large crowd, he had compassion on them, because they were like sheep without a shepherd. So he began teaching them many things.
> *Mark 6:34*

He was primarily concerned with teaching them so they might have a relationship with God and find the true Shepherd.

He also blessed the limited food supply of five loaves and two fish available. The food was multiplied, and He then distributed the food to the crowd, and more than 5,000 people were fed at the one time.

One day He met a widow whose son had just died (Luke 7:11–15). His heart went out to the lady, and in compassion He raised the young man from the dead.

Jesus shows us that God is a God of compassion. There are two key elements of compassion. Firstly, there must be accurate empathy. This involves the ability to sense and understand how the other person is feeling. Jesus shows this supremely. A second component is to have the commitment to seek to do something about the situation. Jesus combines these two qualities in Himself. There is His sensitivity to the person and His particular care for individuals, but also there is the power to bring change in the person's life.

Here is the true story of someone called Anna.

Life was a very lonely, desolate place for me. I was tired of hiding behind a smile while inside I was experiencing gut-wrenching pain. Inside I was dead, and I could no longer hide it, so I hid away in my little house. I thought of just quietly walking into the sea and leaving this world behind. I felt dying was my only way out.

I cried out, 'O, God, I can't take this any more. Please take this pain away.' I stood up to walk out of the door and go to the sea to end it all, when a text message came through on my mobile: 'Hi, thinking about you, how are you?'

I had nothing left to lose, so I responded, 'I'm battling with the will to live.'

My friend responded immediately and gave me the phone number of a counsellor.

Deep down, I didn't want to die. I just wanted the pain to stop, and I could see no other way of stopping it.

I met with the counsellor once a week for six weeks, and each time felt better and better. I felt God's love for me more and more every day. God took away my pain and emptiness and filled me with a comfort and peace I had never felt before.

Do I still want to die? No, a thousand times, No! God has made me a new person, a person who now loves to wake in the morning, wondering what the day will bring and knowing He is right by my side.

(From Graeme Wylie's *Journey to Wellness: A Guide to Spiritual and Emotional Health*).[1]

This power is still available today. The power of Christ can transform our lives. In 2 Corinthians 5:17 we read, 'Therefore, if anyone is in Christ, the new creation has come: The old has gone, the new is here!'

God understands us because He made us. He knows our human condition because He Himself experienced it. He understands the pain and the distress of rejection. He went to a very painful death because of His love for us. But He is also committed to bringing change and restoration to our lives, if we will allow Him to do so. He can make all things new and make us new creations, by giving us a fresh start in our lives. If we come to Him, and confess our need of Him, then He will change us and restore us. We can indeed become new on the inside.

Does this mean that Christians will never become suicidal? No. Christians may still become suicidal, and some Christians have died by suicide. However, as Patricia Casey points out in her research article, 'The psychosocial benefits of religious practice', the numbers tend to be fewer than among those who do not practise their religious beliefs. The reason for this is that Christ gives us hope. He comes into our lives to bring change and restoration and to help us through our difficulties. He is also there beyond the grave, and we look forward to sharing eternity with Him. This is the tremendous Christian hope which we have.

Summary of chapters five and six

- Careful assessment of the person who may be suicidal is very important.

- Helping someone look beyond the immediate crisis can be vital.

- A person may not actually want to die, but is unable to cope with the pain they are experiencing.

- Increasing 'connectedness' for the person, showing compassion and building resilience, are helpful in suicide prevention.

- Discovering the presence and power of Christ can transform a person's experience.

---

[1] Graeme Wylie, *Journey to Wellness: A Guide to Spiritual and Emotional Health*, available from www.chooselife.ie info@hopecounselling.ie (accessed 08/09/2015).

Recommended resources

Courtney Anderson, *To the Golden Shore: The Life of Adoniram Judson* (Valley Forge, PA: Judson Press, 1987).

Chapter seven
The person with addictions

Addiction is a very real problem. There can be many substances to which one can be addicted. Here is an imaginary case scenario.

Carolyn had been smoking for more than 30 years, since being taught by her friend on the school bus. Her father died from lung cancer in his fifties. Her friends managed to quit, and she was able to stop for a year, but then she went back to smoking again. This started because she had put on weight. She tried just stopping completely, and then used nicotine replacement therapy. She finally gave up smoking using a self-help booklet.

She has now been off cigarettes for six months, but she still has an intense desire for a cigarette. She knows this feeling will not go away easily, but it does become a little less every day. The craving is brought on by certain things: walking behind someone in the street who is smoking, or having an argument with her partner. A difficult day at work can really bring it on. Having a glass of wine in the evening can be a trigger. Her first cup of coffee in the morning brings to mind that she wants to have a cigarette. She now tends to avoid parties where a lot of people will be smoking. Having a lot of fruit available helps when she has a desperate desire for a cigarette. She has started exercising in the local park. She still knows that she must take one day at a time, and it can be a real battle.

How do we understand craving?

Craving is not a pleasant feeling. It involves a sense of bodily tension, and anxiety with irritability. One feels as though one is on a short fuse. There is muscle tension, sweating, racing of the heart, light-headedness and headache. These feelings of craving can be more intense when the substance which can relieve them is not available. It often comes on a few hours after the last dose of the substance and can remain for several days. It can be triggered by external cues, such as seeing someone using the substance for which one craves. Also, it can be brought on by internal cues, such as feeling stressed or depressed, or feeling under pressure for some other reason.

How do we recognise dependence?

A scenario I use in training groups to recognise different problems is this one below.

You are part of a team helping people late at night on the street. You meet a man called Noel, a man in his late fifties who is a bit dishevelled in his appearance. He is sweaty, and his hands are trembling. He tells you his name but also appears confused. He does not seem to quite make sense. He says he has an occasional drink every now and then. He mentions that he had a few drinks yesterday but can't say exactly when this was.

Noel's condition is worrying. He is quite agitated. You sit him down and try to talk to him. Someone brings over a cup of coffee. You ask him a few more questions. He seems quite jumpy. Although he is able to say he drinks a bit, he does not make very much sense. You are concerned about how much he is shaking, and you feel that it might be better if you could arrange for him to see a doctor. You are worried he might collapse. You decide to call an ambulance, and you go to hospital with him. The doctor sees him, and finds his old records. It seems that Noel has been a heavy drinker for many years and has a condition called alcohol dependence. He is in the early stages of withdrawal. Usually he manages to get some cheap cider at the local supermarket to cope with the withdrawal, but today he has run out of money, or so his brother Joe says, whom the doctor has managed to contact. Joe also says that Noel has had a condition before called delirium tremens, where he becomes very confused and can be aggressive. The last time he had this he was seeing hundreds of spiders crawling around him and was very frightened.

How do we understand dependence?

There are six key factors of dependence:

- Firstly, there is a compulsion to take the substance.

- Secondly, people are unable to control their habit of taking the particular substance.

- Thirdly, there is often a withdrawal state from the substance. This withdrawal state can be very unpleasant, and will vary depending on the substance taken.

- Fourthly, it tends to be the case that people take more and more of the substance for the same effect. This is referred to as tolerance.

- Fifthly, the substance tends to take over the whole of life.

- Sixthly, if after a period of abstinence the substance is retaken then the whole cycle tends to repeat itself.

Noel has shown all of these features and is dependent on alcohol.

Joe tells you that Noel used to be a salesman for a large clothing firm. He would often be taking out prospective clients for a meal in the evenings. Frequently there would be a fair amount of wine flowing. Then it got to the stage that Noel could not manage without having a drink every day, and usually it ended up being a bottle, sometimes two, of wine every evening. He then found he got shaky in the mornings and had to have a drink to calm him down sufficiently to get to work. Then the inevitable happened. One evening he had a small road traffic accident and when the police breathalysed him, he was way over the limit. He lost his licence and with it, his job. That was five years ago and he has not worked since. Now he finds he cannot manage without the drink, but money is tighter and he is on cheap cider. Today he couldn't even get that, and he is now in a state of acute withdrawal.

When one is in a state of dependence, the substance tends to take over one's whole life. A person tends to neglect important areas of life in order to obtain the substance. This can affect finances, family life, employment and all kinds of other areas. The substance is now in control of the person, rather than the person being in control of the substance. The person tends to take the substance in a continuing way, despite ongoing evidence of harm.

Noel knows he is dependent on alcohol, but finds he cannot stop drinking. He managed it for a month or so, about four years back. At that stage, his wife, Dorothy, told him that he would have to stop, or else she could not cope any longer. Noel sometimes became violent after a drinking bout, and on one occasion hit Dorothy, giving her a nasty black eye, which not only hurt, but gave her a bad day at work with all the comments she received from her colleagues. With some pills from the doctor, he managed to get free from the alcohol for a month, but after a hard day he relapsed into his old ways. He even stole Dorothy's jewellery to pay for the drink, and finally she could take no more and moved out to her daughter's home. Now they meet occasionally, but divorce proceedings have begun. Alcohol has completely taken over his life. Noel just lives for the next drink. The doctor told him that he will be lucky to live out the next couple of years and his liver is badly affected. Also he was vomiting blood not long ago, but Noel still cannot stop the drinking.

How do we consider addiction?

There is a difference between substances in their addictive potential. Some substances are much more addictive than others. For example, a large proportion of people using nicotine or cocaine become addicted. However, most people can tolerate a glass of wine or two without becoming addicted. In Noel's case it was about three years from drinking to excess in the evenings to the realisation that he was dependent on the alcohol and could not manage without it on a daily basis.

Once addicted, people can have major difficulties in trying to stop taking the substance. For example, of smokers attempting to give up, only 15 per cent remain abstinent after 52 weeks.[1] Many teenagers who smoke will be trapped in a cycle of regular smoking that lasts up to 30 or 40 years. Stopping smoking can be very difficult.

How do we understand the addictive process and its effect on our bodies?

The human brain is amazingly complex. At the front of the brain behind the forehead is the decision-making and executive centre. Deep within the brain there is what is called the 'reward pathway'. This pathway, when triggered, releases a substance called dopamine. This gives a pleasurable feeling in the individual in response to such things as food and sexual contact. This release of dopamine is also triggered by alcohol, nicotine, heroin, cocaine and other substances. Taking the substance brings relaxation, or a pleasant state. However, continuing to take the substance can cause addiction. There is good evidence that addiction to pornography also uses this reward pathway. The person who becomes addicted wants the substance or stimulus because of the pleasant effects, but realises the difficulties in continuing with their particular behavioural pattern.

Now, we might consider there is a fight going on between the front of the brain, which believes that taking a substance is not a good idea, and the deeper part of the brain where the dopamine is released through the reward pathway, bringing a pleasurable sensation. This fight in the brain is something that people who are addicted to substances continually experience. They wish to take the substance because of the pleasant effects, but they understand, at some level, the damage that they are doing to their bodily systems. The longer the person persists in taking the substance, the more difficult it becomes to desist. The front of the brain is telling the person to stop taking the substance because of the serious problems that will follow. The reward centre is saying, 'I like the effects of this substance and want to continue taking it.' So there is a fight in the brain between the frontal area and the reward pathway that releases dopamine.

What are the main problems with alcohol?

During my previous visits to medical wards as a psychiatrist, I was often asked to see people who were in the acute stages of alcohol withdrawal. They were frequently in a very serious condition.

Whilst Noel, the person you had met in the street, was in the emergency department, he started to have quite a serious seizure. It was good that the doctors were on hand, and they were able to turn him into the recovery position so that when he vomited afterwards, at least he didn't inhale the vomit. He was moved up to the ward, and an intravenous line was inserted to give him fluids and vitamins. Over the next few days he was very disturbed and pulled out the line on two or three occasions. He was given a lot of sedation. Despite this, he nearly punched the doctor who was called to replace the intravenous line. When Noel finally came round, after about three days or so, he seemed very low and down. He was beginning to see again what a mess he had made of his life through the drink.

Alcohol has major effects on the body. As we noted earlier, many people do not realise that alcohol is actually a depressant. In other words, if someone is depressed and they take alcohol, they are likely to become more depressed. It also changes the person's ability to solve problems. A person, having taken alcohol, is much less likely to be able to solve difficulties. It also increases impulsiveness. This may be shown in aggressive outbursts, but also, more worryingly, in the fact that around one-third of suicides involve alcohol. The person who has died by suicide has often seemed to have acted in an impulsive manner, and this may have been triggered by alcohol ingestion. Plus, alcohol creates dependency. It can also be directly toxic. Someone who has never taken alcohol before and ingests a huge quantity may be killed directly by the toxic effects. Alcohol is involved in some way or other in the deaths of 25 per cent of 15- to 29-year-old males.

Are there any safe limits to alcohol ingestion?

There are suggested limits. This does not mean that somebody who takes less than this limit will never have any problems with alcohol, but there are limits that one should not exceed. When considering alcohol ingestion, we talk about units. Half a glass of wine, half a pint of beer or a single measure of spirits is considered to be one unit. Proposed new guidelines in the UK suggest limits for both men and women of 14 units per week.[2] If one exceeds these limits, then the risks of alcohol-related damage increase. If one is also a heavy smoker, these risks are further increased.

How may alcohol affect our bodies?

It affects the liver and may lead to cirrhosis (scarring of the liver), hepatitis and liver cancer. Pancreatitis (inflammation of the pancreas) is often a severe and very painful illness and can be related to alcohol ingestion. Alcohol is related to cancers of the mouth, throat and oesophagus. Many people with alcohol problems have ulcers in the stomach, and blood loss may result from these. There are other causes of blood loss, also related to alcohol. In Noel's case, he had cirrhosis of the liver, and this had caused the veins in the lower end of his oesophagus to become very swollen and prone to bleed. This is the reason he had vomited blood previously.

I used to see many people with alcohol problems who had brain damage or dementia. The brain damage can be of different kinds. There may be a marked loss of memory and they may make up stories to cover up for this memory loss. This is part of the illness called Wernicke-Korsakoff's syndrome.

Other people who drink heavily have developed a frank dementia. In this condition there is not only progressive memory loss, but also the loss of ability to look after oneself and to function independently. Head injury is common in people with alcohol problems, which again can lead to ongoing difficulties.

Vitamin deficiencies are very common. Deficiencies of B vitamins are well recognised. Seizures and epilepsy may become problems for people with heavy alcohol abuse. Seizures, on acute withdrawal from alcohol, are not uncommon, and this is what happened to Noel in the emergency department. There may be walking and balance problems. There is often an increased rate of heart disease and high blood pressure.

What about the pregnant mother who is drinking heavily?

There can be harm to the unborn baby. The so-called foetal alcohol syndrome can cause serious problems in infancy and also in later life, directly related to alcohol ingestion during pregnancy. Alcohol can also cause stillbirth and low birth weight.

What further mental health and social consequences may be related to excess alcohol ingestion?

The person who drinks heavily may become depressed, or indeed someone with depression might drink heavily as a way of coping with depression. There can also be deterioration in the personality. There can be sexual difficulties related to alcohol. One condition that can arise is called 'pathological jealousy', or alternatively the Othello syndrome, after the Shakespearean character. This is not uncommon in those who have alcohol dependence. The individual tends to imagine that the other person in relationship with them is having an affair with someone else. The person may go to extreme lengths to try to corroborate these incorrect beliefs, and to prove infidelity in the partner. Hallucinations can occur in alcoholism, often in the manner of insults or threats to the person even when they are fully conscious. Then there are problems of increased accidents, crime, family breakdown and partner battery. The list of potential problems is relatively endless.

What are the signs of alcohol withdrawal?

Someone who is withdrawing from alcohol may have tremor of the hands, particularly in the mornings. Usually there is evidence of recent early morning drinking. There may be agitation, nausea, retching or sweating. There can be misperceptions and hallucinations.

In the serious condition of delirium tremens, there is often shaking of the limbs, or seizures, although these are usually preventable if skilled medical help is available. The individual is often out of touch with reality. The person can believe that they are being persecuted and may have visual hallucinations. In these, it is not uncommon that the person sees small objects – mice or rats or insects – that are not actually there. With these visual hallucinations there is often severe agitation and fear. Noel had had this before and had been terrified by the experience. On this occasion he did not have the full picture of delirium tremens owing to skilful and timely intervention from the medical team. Often the person with delirium tremens can be medically very ill, and sometimes may die.

Acute alcohol withdrawal requires skilled treatment. One needs to give a tranquilliser such as Librium, often in high doses, to stop the very severe withdrawal effects. One also prescribes high-dose vitamins to treat potential or actual vitamin deficiencies and to prevent further complications.

How can we understand drug abuse and dependence?

You meet a young man called Peter coming out of a club in the city centre. He seems a bit excitable and also might be in pain. You get talking to him. You notice he has a runny nose and dilated pupils. He seems a bit twitchy and complains of muscle cramps and feeling cold, despite the warm weather. Apart from this, he looks in fairly good physical shape. He says he feels really bad and wants some money. He thinks you are a Christian, and also tells you that he is truly ready to turn his life around if he's just given a chance. He now needs some money urgently so he can get a taxi home.

He denies any drug abuse, but you are suspicious. A girl called Kirsty is with him, and you see her motioning to Claire, who is on the street team with you that night. Kirsty says to Claire, 'Don't give Peter any money; he will just spend it on drugs.' Claire invites her for a coffee on the team bus, while you carry on talking to Peter. Kirsty says, 'I am so worried about Peter. He is a great guy, and I have known him for the last five years, but it's the drugs that have got him. He's now just 19. It started with cannabis, and he was taking it every day at 15. Then he got in with the wrong crowd. His mum did not notice at first. He had been doing very well at school, and then he just stopped studying and spent all his time in his room. He completely flunked his GCSEs even though he is so clever. Then his mum noticed money going missing in the house, and she confronted him about this. Well, there was a nasty row and he moved out to his friend's place. There was a bad crowd there. He was on cocaine at one stage, but I think he might be off that now. They slipped stuff in his drink one day, and he blacked out and woke up in hospital. The doctor said it had been a close shave. And then he moved back home for a while, but his mum found some needles on the floor. He'd started on heroin. He's been on it now for the last two years and he won't get help. I'm so worried about him. I think he's having a withdrawal reaction now, and I'm so concerned. But there's no point in giving him money. It will just go towards the next fix. He's beginning to take greater and greater amounts. He needs to take more and more for the same effect. He cannot stop taking drugs. He cannot think of anything else. He's spending all his money on them. He's now begun to steal even his mum's jewellery, to sell it so that he can buy his drugs. He even sold his guitar, which he used to love playing. I don't know why I stick with him, really, but he has so few friends left, and I desperately want him to get help. Do you think you could get help for him?' she asks plaintively.

Drug abuse is a serious problem. In England two per cent of 11-year-old children will have taken drugs in the last month and five per cent will have taken them in the previous year. At the age of 15, the figures will have risen to 14 per cent having taken drugs in the last month and 25 per cent in the last year. There is good evidence that drug-taking amongst young people is actually now falling in England.[3] Risks of drug abuse are higher in those who smoke. Drug dependency tends to be higher in those who are living rough and those in prison.

Why do people take drugs?

There can be many reasons. Some will take them for pleasure, enjoyment and excitement. As mentioned, the release of dopamine in the reward centre leads to a state of pleasure and enjoyment. At times people will take drugs as a way of escaping from difficult and stressful situations. Drugs may be taken to deal with sorrow and deep disappointment. Alternatively, as with Peter, they may be taken as a way of celebration and to feel socially accepted by others. His friends started taking cannabis, and he wanted to be one of the crowd, so he started taking it too. People may also take drugs as a way of dealing with boredom.

Some may take drugs to cope with withdrawal symptoms. For instance, if one becomes addicted to a drug and then experiences severe withdrawal symptoms, one looks for the drug again, to deal with these symptoms. This was the case with Peter. He had been on heroin for some time, and he knew what it was like to go into severe withdrawal. He had sometimes run out of money, but then he had become desperate for another 'fix'. Similarly, if craving is a real problem, then drugs are taken to deal with the craving. Some take drugs as a way of dealing with depression and low self-esteem. Others take drugs as a way of increasing confidence. They may be taken to relieve other psychological, psychiatric and physical symptoms. Some may take them as a way of dealing with physical pain. As doctors, we find that some people are given prescription drugs for severe pain, but in the end, if one is not careful, the person may become dependent on these strong analgesics. Sometimes people take drugs as a way of increasing energy and concentration, or to enhance performance. They may be taken to lose weight, to unwind, or simply just to have fun.

Are there protective factors which will help prevent somebody from abusing drugs?

There are several of these. If there are secure early relationships in the family, these can be very helpful. In

Peter's case, there had been disruption of his family when he was a child.

Peter's father had walked out several years before, and for a while his mum had been so depressed she had found it hard to look after Peter. Peter's older sister had had to try to cope with her mum's depression and Peter's tendency to be quite wild as a young teenager. Relationships in the whole family had been quite strained.

Good relationships in the family are important. If there is a good relationship with at least one parent, this is protective. If the family shows affection and demonstrates reasonable discipline, again these are protective factors. If there is a relative lack of family strife, this can be important. If the family tends to support the need for education, this is protective. If parents show disapproval of drugs, then this is helpful and preventative. Females are generally less likely to become dependent on drugs than males. Intelligence is a protective factor. Having a positive attitude in life is important. Good communication skills are valuable. If someone is able to say why they are taking drugs, or can discuss their underlying problems, this can be helpful. If there is a general problem-solving approach to difficulties in life, this can be useful. Supportive networks of friends and relations tend to be protective. A higher standard of living is often protective. In regard to schooling, in those schools that provide a large range of opportunities, drug abuse tends to be lower. Sporting activities can also be valuable.

Are there ways of detecting drug misuse?

There are several warning signs. Sometimes there can be a marked decline in school or work performance that is worrying. This was the case with Peter. From being nearly the best in his class, his academic performance had gone into free-fall, and he had only managed a bare pass in three subjects at GCSE. There may be unexplained mood changes. The person may show evasive or secretive behaviour. Peter had spent long hours by himself, had sometimes appeared 'spaced out', and then his mother had noticed money going missing. This is what finally alerted her to Peter's drug problem. The person may seem to 'lose' possessions or money, since these are being used to obtain drugs. A drug user may turn to stealing and other crime to fund the habit. They may lose friends, or be secretive about new friends. Changes in routine can be present. If there is excessive drowsiness or overactivity, this can be a cause for concern. Again, if there is evidence of deteriorating appearance or poor health, then these are worrying signs.

How can one respond if drug abuse is suspected?

First of all, it is good to be well-informed. There are many helpful websites where information can be gained about different drugs and their effects. These can help parents to know whether their teenager is taking drugs. Parents should not be afraid to talk to a young person about their concerns. However, it is better to do this when the teenager is sober and not under the influence of drugs. Also it can be valuable to get support and help from others. It may be necessary to talk to someone else in confidence about the problem. It is not a good idea just to leave it and hope the problem will go away. It is important to show care by actually talking about the drug issue.

What are the adverse physical and mental effects of drugs?

This depends on the actual drug involved and the extent to which it is being misused. Drug abuse can lead to new forms of mental illness, and existing mental illness can become much worse.

There are physical signs of drug misuse. If there is intravenous use of the drug, then there may be infection, or possibly damaged blood vessels, with perhaps the evidence of 'tramlines' on the arms or legs, which have been sites of intravenous injection, where the veins have hardened. HIV and hepatitis and other physical health problems may ensue.

There may be signs of a withdrawal state. Withdrawal states from drugs can vary depending on the drug used. However, there can be depression and suicidal feelings particularly after withdrawal from stimulant drugs. There can be marked confusion following withdrawal from alcohol or similar substances. If a mother using heroin gives birth, the baby may then show withdrawal effects. Drugs may also affect an unborn child's growth and development.

What are some of the social effects of drug abuse?

In terms of social changes, drug abuse may lead to adverse consequences such as unemployment, crime and neglect of family.

Peter had moved out of home, and had never had a proper job. He was claiming benefits and trying to earn a bit on the side by doing some furniture lifting with a friend who had a van. He was also stealing, when he could manage it, to sustain his habit. The police had been after him at one stage and had cautioned him, but had not actually arrested him.

Other social problems that drug users may fall into are expulsion from school, and then potentially later, homelessness, prostitution, conviction and prison sentences.

In this next section, I am not attempting to give a full account of drug dependency problems, but rather to offer a few illustrative examples.

What effects does heroin have?

The person often feels sleepy, relaxed and content. However, there may be constipation or reduced appetite and reduced interest in sex. The person may become drowsy, and breathing and heart rate tend to slow down. It often takes a while to become physically dependent. In Peter's case, he had used heroin intermittently at first. It was only in the last year that he had become fully addicted.

Tolerance had occurred, where a person takes an increased amount of the substance to gain the same effect. There is a high risk of overdose with heroin. If someone has been taking a high dose of the drug, stops taking it for a period of time and then, after this time lapse, takes the same dose again, this can prove fatal.

Peter's girlfriend, Kirsty, said that his heroin dose had been going up and up. However, for a few days he had gone with her to meet her parents in the country and she was sure he was not taking it then. She was so upset when, coming back to town, she saw him with the syringe again. By this stage she had read up quite a bit about heroin and knew the risks of taking the same amount after being off it for a while, and although she could not stop him taking it, she was able to persuade him to take only half the usual amount. She is hoping at least now to get him to the clinic to get him on methadone (a heroin substitute) instead, with the hope that he will finally be able to get off drugs completely. Kirsty looks a bit forlorn whilst saying this. It seems that she does not feel very hopeful.

Withdrawal from heroin causes dilated pupils, restlessness, shakiness, inability to sleep, stomach cramps, vomiting and diarrhoea, runny eyes and nose, hot and cold sweats and intense cravings. There is a high risk of suicide with addiction to heroin.

What about substitute prescribing?

Substitute prescribing with methadone is considered safer than continuance with heroin. There are fewer risks from dirty needles, and reduced problems with crime. Since the methadone is provided freely there is, in theory, no longer the need to steal to obtain the drug. The dose can also be more accurately measured. However, methadone is not without its problems and can make its way on to the drugs' black market. Some also have an ethical difficulty with substituting one substance which causes addiction with another, since methadone produces very similar effects to heroin.

What is cannabis, and what effects does it have?

Cannabis is available as dried vegetation called grass or marijuana, or as a resin. The effects of it are that the person will often feel happy and sleepy. There is often a sense of distortion of space and time. There may be red eyes and increased appetite. The individual may, however, become anxious and agitated or show disturbed behaviour. They may have hallucinations and become paranoid (an extreme or irrational fear or distrust of others).

When I first went into psychiatry, one of my initial experiences was working as a doctor in the East End of London. Here on an average weekend I would admit several people to hospital, usually young males, who had severe cannabis intoxication and were very paranoid. I would find that on future admissions some of these people, who had initially presented with a paranoid state and marked intoxication as a result of cannabis, would have an illness that was indistinguishable from schizophrenia. There have now been several studies which show that cannabis (particularly skunk – a strong-smelling and more potent form) is a risk factor for the development of schizophrenia. It can also result in somebody becoming very apathetic and unmotivated. We refer to this as an 'amotivational' state. Cannabis can cause dependence in some people. Others may become depressed. There can be a withdrawal state with anxiety, sweating and muscle aches.

What are stimulants, and what effects may they have?

Stimulants such as cocaine can cause strong dependence. Initially, following ingestion, there is excitement and euphoria, and the person may have exaggerated belief in their own importance and abilities. Those using them may become sexually disinhibited. There are often hallucinations, and users may become very paranoid. Violent and aggressive outbursts may occur. They are often extremely agitated. There is frequently an increase in pulse rate and blood pressure, and they may present with fits or even a stroke, or occasional sudden death. Following ingestion of the stimulant they often 'crash' with severe depression, suicidal thoughts and intense craving for the drug.

Are there any medications that can be given for addictions?

Nicotine replacement therapy can be valuable for smokers. Recently e-cigarettes (which electronically deliver nicotine) have been used widely. They can be helpful for people who are smoking heavily. Nicotine may also be prescribed in various other ways. The aim is to bring about a gradual reduction in nicotine consumption.

In alcohol problems, medications can sometimes be given with the aim of reducing the risk of relapse by reducing the strength and frequency of craving.

In those dependent on heroin, substitutes such as methadone may be prescribed. With those addicted to minor tranquillisers, gradually using smaller amounts of these can be a way of weaning them off from heavy use.

Can 'talking' therapies help?

There are different kinds of 'talking' treatments that may help. CBT is useful because it concentrates on the way people think and the mistakes that they may be making in their thinking. Here the person is helped to recognise their thought patterns which may be negative and incorrect. If these patterns can be changed, then this can help to change the emotions and then the behaviour. Negative emotions often lead to the taking of a drug or alcohol in an attempt to try to resolve the unpleasant emotional state. If, however, the negative thought patterns preceding the negative emotions can be identified and challenged, then the cycle may be prevented. CBT tends to focus on the 'here and now' difficulties that the person is experiencing.

Motivational Enhancement Therapy helps people to make positive changes. In this therapy, an individual is helped to understand the balance between the risks and benefits of their current behaviour. Then they may be helped towards making decisions that will be beneficial in the long term. For example, confronted with the dangers and effects of alcohol on the body, can the individual be helped towards becoming motivated to take a decision to stop taking the alcohol, or if not, helped to reduce the drinking to a safer level?

Relapse Prevention helps people identify situations that could lead to relapse. For example, it might be important to help the person recognise the triggers that could lead to a relapse. Avoiding going to parties where drugs are freely available can be prudent. Carrying a card with all the reasons why the person decided to stop taking the drug or substance can be valuable. Then, in a crisis situation, pulling out the card and going through it can be helpful in avoiding beginning to take the substance again.

In what further ways can people be helped to overcome addictive behaviour?

One of the difficulties with many substances of abuse, in particular alcohol, is that once free from the substance, taking it again can quickly lead back into the same cycle of addiction. Distraction can be helpful to many people. For example, if one is tempted to take the substance, switching to a different activity such as exercise, watching a film or reading a book can be useful as a way of turning away from the immediate temptation. Likewise, talking the problem through can be helpful. Alternatively, talking about something completely different can also help. Learning relaxation techniques (such as muscular relaxation or breathing techniques) as a way of dealing with stress and pressure, rather than taking drugs, can also be beneficial. Many people find that support groups are vital for them.

Alcoholics Anonymous is very helpful for many. Al-Anon can help the family and friends of those with alcohol problems, and Narcotics Anonymous can also be beneficial. There are many self-help groups available. There are also several phone helplines available. Short-term residential placements can help some people break the cycle of addiction.

How may religious practice have an impact on drug abuse and dependence?

Again, the work of Professor Patricia Casey is valuable here. In her examination of more than 300 papers linking together mental health and religious practice, she showed that in young people who practised their religious faith there was a lower level of use of drugs and alcohol.

[1] L. Bauld, K. Bell, L. McCullough et al, 'The effectiveness of NHS smoking cessation services: a systematic review'. *Journal of Public Health* 32: 71-82 (2010).
[2] UK Chief Medical Officer's Alcohol Guidelines Review: Summary of the proposed new guidelines. January 2016. Available at www.gov.uk (accessed 8th January 2016).
[3] Statistics on Drug Misuse – England, 2011 www.hscic.gov.uk/pubs/drugmisuse11 (accessed 8th September 2015).

Recommended resources

A selection of helplines available:

- Drinkaware (advice on alcohol): 0300 123 1110.

- Talk to Frank (drugs information and advice line): 0300 123 6600.

- Al-Anon (help for families affected by someone else's drinking): 020 7403 0888.

- Alcoholics Anonymous (help for those with alcohol problems): 0800 9177 650.

- Addiction Helper (guide to alcohol and drug rehabilitation centres): 0203 553 6494.

- Narcotics Anonymous (help for those affected by a drug problem): 0300 999 1212.

(numbers correct as of 3rd September 2015)

Chapter eight
Spiritual help in addictions

What spiritual help is available to assist a person to become free from addiction?

One of the heroes of the Christian faith has been William Booth. At the age of 13 he was apprenticed to a pawnbroker because his father could no longer afford his school fees. He was out of work for a year and then moved to London to work in a pawnbroker's shop. In 1865 he began his work amongst the neediest of London's East End. He was a passionate preacher and his wife, Catherine, described how he would come home night after night, completely exhausted, with his clothes torn and his face bandaged from where he had been struck by stones.

In the East End of London at the end of the nineteenth century the situation for many men and women was pitiful. Despite the fact that Britain had a large empire, the state in which people lived in that part of London was deplorable. Prostitution was rife, as was alcohol abuse. Alcohol was freely available, and the rate of alcoholism was high.

William Booth believed in the power of God to set a person free. He would bring people into a powerful revival meeting. There they would find the presence and power of God. However, he did not stop there, but did his utmost to find people employment. He recognised that a man needed to regain dignity and a sense of importance and value, and for this, work was necessary. He also recognised that sometimes the environment was unhelpful. With this in mind, he established farms in the country or even, later on, abroad. To my knowledge, the rates of his success have rarely been equalled. A large majority of people who came off alcohol remained off it. His book *In Darkest England and the Way Out*, first published in 1890, is still well worth reading.

Alcoholics Anonymous (AA) and its 12-step programme has been a powerful resource of help to many thousands of people. Bill Wilson and Dr Robert Smith, its co-founders, both had a strong Christian faith, and many people have found a real experience of God through AA and its 12 steps, as well as release from alcohol dependence. The key message is that people are unable to conquer alcoholism by themselves. They are encouraged to surrender to a higher power and to be in conversation with other alcoholics about their difficulties. This is usually arranged through regular meetings in the locality. The book *Alcoholics Anonymous*, enshrining these principles, was written by Bill Wilson in 1939 and is often referred to as 'The Big Book'.

When it comes to the problems of drug abuse, in particular heroin abuse, the story of Jackie Pullinger, who has been based in Hong Kong, is similarly inspiring. At a young age she wanted to be a missionary, but was uncertain how to proceed. Although the advice she was given was somewhat unusual, Richard Thompson, a minister in Shoreditch, London, encouraged her to get onto a ship and to pray to know when to get off the boat. She finally ended up in Hong Kong, in 1966. Initially, it was difficult to gain entrance to the country, but her mother's godson was a police officer there so she was able to stay and find employment as a primary school teacher in Kowloon Walled City. This place was one of the world's largest opium-producing centres. Here there were many people addicted to heroin. With some of her assistants, she helped these people to go 'cold turkey'. However, during the withdrawal experience the person always had somebody with them, who prayed for them intensely. Many people came off drugs successfully and have remained free of drugs since then. A number of these now help others who are similarly addicted.

Teen Challenge is a movement in many countries started in 1958 by David Wilkerson, a preacher and pastor who worked on the streets of New York with members of rival street gangs. Teen Challenge has many residential centres where help is given to those addicted to drugs. The programmes focus on the recognition of destructive thought patterns that may lead to drug abuse. They aim to help people to recognise and find help for past failures and broken relationships. Spiritual growth and character development are encouraged. They help people with future plans and help them reintegrate into society. Several studies have shown significant benefits from these programmes.[1]

What is the addictive process, and what are the ways through?

In our discussions so far, we have mentioned the fight in the brain between the reward pathway which releases dopamine, and the front part of the brain which has executive function. Understanding this fight can be useful in thinking about how to help people with drug and alcohol abuse and dependence. We need to understand that a person's body and mind become enslaved by the addictive substance. The substance has become all-important and is controlling the person. This control effect of the substance can be seen in the way that a person's finances, marriage and, indeed, all aspects of life can become dominated by the need to obtain and use the drug. This takes precedence over all other activities in life. However, as a result of this continued behaviour, a person often feels guilty and finds it difficult to have a relationship with God.

The Bible pictures us all in a condition of slavery. Jesus said, 'Very truly I tell you, everyone who sins is a slave to sin' (John 8:34). In the person who is addicted, this slavery can be understood as occurring when a substance effectively takes over the person's life.

However, there is no slavery that cannot be broken by His power. He says, 'So if the Son sets you free, you will be free indeed' (John 8:36). He has the power to transform our lives, and set us free from slavery and patterns of addiction.

The Bible also says:

160

> In the same way, count yourselves dead to sin, but alive
> to God in Christ Jesus. Therefore do not let sin reign in
> your mortal body so that you obey its evil desires ... For
> sin shall no longer be your master.
>
> *Romans 6:11–12, 14*

These verses tell us that sin no longer needs to have dominion over us, that we can indeed be free. How does this work practically in our lives?

Imagine for a moment that you have spent many years in the army. Automatically, on a daily basis, you have saluted your commandant. Then you leave the army, and you meet your commandant in the street. Your automatic reaction is to want to salute. However, now you don't have to respond in this way because you are no longer in the army and your relationship with him has changed. In the same way, those who have been addicted, when presented with the substance to which they have been addicted, may feel that they have no other response but to 'salute' the drug and obey the desires it brings. Through the freedom that Christ supplies, this is no longer necessary. However, the reality also is that the faster we turn away from this very obvious source of temptation, the more likely we are to succeed in overcoming it.

The person may be abusing drugs to fill an inner void. St Augustine said, 'You have made us for Yourself, O Lord, and our heart is restless until it rests in You.'[2] There is a restless void inside a human being that can only be filled by the Spirit of the living God. Without this we are spiritually empty, and we will try to fill this inner emptiness with all kinds of things in an attempt to dull the pain of the emptiness. As we look to Christ for His power and deliverance, He can fill us with the Holy Spirit. The story below illustrates the power of the Holy Spirit in our lives to break the chains of addiction and set us free, filling us with new joy and peace.

Here is the true story of a lady we will call Jane. She had two young daughters at the time of this story:

In Ireland I soon adopted alcohol into my diet of drugs. I got into such a state that I was spending all my money on drink and drugs and relying on friends to feed the girls and me. We spent almost every day in the pub. A crisis came for me when I had an accident at a party. I cut myself badly and had to get stitched up at the hospital. When I got back home to the girls they said, 'Mum, you could have killed yourself!', and it was like a light going on. I realised what a mess I had become and knew I had to do something about it.

The only thing I could think of was a friend who used to hang around the Galway hippie scene telling everyone about Jesus. I thought, seeing I had tried everything else, I might as well give Him a shot, so I agreed to go to a 'prayer meeting' with my friend. This was the turning point of my whole life, the spiritual awakening I had been searching for since my teenage years.

As I walked into the prayer meeting, I sensed these people had something I lacked. They looked so happy, and their eyes were shining. With their guidance, I asked God to forgive my sins through Jesus, and then I received prayer to be filled with the Holy Spirit.

At that moment I experienced a power that I had never encountered before. I felt fire travel through my body, and my knees buckled under me. I was filled with the most incredible love and peace. In that moment I knew without a doubt that Jesus was alive!

The change was so dramatic that my old hippie friends used to stop me in the street to ask me what had happened! A few years later God gave me a husband, and I have been happily married with five wonderful children for the last 16 years.

(From Graeme Wylie's *Journey to Wellness: A Guide to Spiritual and Emotional Health*).[3]

What other emotional factors can keep a person in a pattern of addictive behaviour?

We need to recognise that most people do not find freedom from addictions in such a dramatic manner. Many people with addictive problems find they keep on falling into the same addiction. Here is a question that a person might need to consider: 'Just before the pattern of behaviour began, what was on my mind?' It could have been a sense of disappointment, grief, failure, or a similar negative thought. The person might be able to understand that they used the substance as a way of trying to deal with the underlying pain and difficulty that they were experiencing.

This is not an uncommon scenario. The difficult emotions of fear, anxiety, emptiness, discouragement, failure and frustration can become the driving forces behind the behaviour. These patterns of behaviour and these difficult negative emotions can arise from problems in the past, from which we have tried to hide or run away. For example, there may be some emotional hurt or damage that happened to us in childhood, or early in life, that has never been fully resolved. Finding the source of the original emotional pain can be helpful. Then the person can be helped to see how they have interpreted this negative and difficult experience.

What was believed as a result of this experience? For example, a sexually abused person may believe the lie that they were to blame, and may feel worthless and dirty as a result of the sexual violation. It can be seen that if these beliefs persist they can cause persistent negative emotions. When one finds the difficult and painful experience, then bringing this into the light through psychotherapy, or during prayer ministry, can be releasing. The power of Christ is available not only to guide and direct our lives in the present, but also to help resolve the effects of the past. It is important to find His help in resolving past traumas and painful memories and the lies associated with these which we have believed. This may prove to be the key to breaking the power of addictions in the present. Jesus can heal the past. He wants to forgive us. He wants to break the power of addictions in our lives, and He wants to heal every part of our being.

Summary of chapters seven and eight

- Understanding the effects and dangers of different drugs and alcohol can be extremely important.

- An understanding of the reward system gives insight into the struggles of those with addictions.

- There are various forms of treatment available, both secular and Christian.

- The ongoing battle with addictions may lead people into a condition of 'slavery' to the addictive substance.

- An awareness of inner emptiness and need may lead a person to look for spiritual help.

---

[1] Study from Teen Challenge of Rehrersburg, Pennsylvania. www.teenchallengeusa.com (accessed 3rd September 2015).
[2] Augustine of Hippo *Confessions* 1,1
[3] Graeme Wylie's *Journey to Wellness: A Guide to Spiritual and Emotional Health*).

Chapter nine
The person with schizophrenia

As mentioned, I have been involved in giving training to an organisation called Street Pastors. As part of the training, I ask them to consider the following case scenario.

Late at night, imagine you are part of a team of people trying to help people from night clubs get home safely. Here is the story of one person walking the streets.

Elaine is 42 years old. On the streets she is pushing a shopping trolley full of her possessions – some rather dirty clothing in plastic bags, and a few newspapers. She appears to be in a dishevelled state. Her shoes are dilapidated and falling apart. She is wearing a stained cardigan and a skirt more suitable for the summer. It is now November, and it is raining hard but she wears no coat. You talk to her to see if she needs help. She starts by telling you that there is a man who says nasty things about her. He lives in the flat next door, and his name is Bert. 'He has been saying, "Get out, you don't belong here." Last night he had a friend in,' she says. 'I heard him. He was saying to his friend, "I'll get rid of the old witch."' She now hears him constantly. She says, 'I can even hear him now. He won't stop.' She covers her ears. 'He's saying he is going to get me. He says he is going to beat me up. I am scared. I had to get out. And even now he won't leave me alone.'

Elaine is very distressed by these experiences and that is why she is walking the streets. It does not seem to bother her that she is wet through and has no coat. You offer her a cup of tea and a seat on the team bus that is parked nearby. You call over one of your helpers. 'Susan, I wonder if you can help this woman?' you ask. 'She has been walking the streets and is absolutely soaked. Can you get her any spare clothing and a coat?' Elaine is shivering quite badly now. You put on the gas ring to make some tea and she holds out her hands to the warmth. You try to find out a bit more about her.

'How long has this man been causing you problems?' you query.

'A long time,' she answers.

'Do you have anyone in your family that we can call to see if they can help you?'

'Well, I do have a sister, but I haven't seen her for quite some time,' she says. She finds her number on a scrap of paper, and tells you that you can telephone her.

Her sister, Beatrice, tells you more of the story. 'Thanks for ringing me,' she says. 'Yes, it is a while since I saw Elaine. The last time I saw her she told me to get out of her house, and she didn't want to see me again. So, yes, it is about three months since I saw her.'

You ask, 'How has she been? What are her problems?'

Beatrice adds, 'When she was 25 she had a bad breakdown and was in hospital for quite a long time – about nine months, it was, in the end. Just before she was discharged, the doctor called me in to meet him and informed me that she was much better, but the illness could come back. He explained that Elaine had become convinced that she could hear people talking about her, and even the television seemed to be making comments about her. He said it was very important that she kept taking the tablets he was prescribing. I asked him what the tablets were, and he said they were called "antipsychotics". I didn't understand so I asked him what they were for. He explained that they were to help keep her thoughts clear and to help her stop hearing the voices. Well, Elaine has never been keen on tablets. She managed to get back to her job as a shop assistant for a short while, but then she stopped taking the tablets, and she was back in hospital about a year later. Since then she hasn't really had any kind of steady job. She stays on the tablets for a while, but then stops them, and she has been back in hospital two or three times. The doctor did recommend a monthly injection instead of the tablets, and she was getting this through a clinic run by a psychiatric nurse called Danny. Here, I have his number – maybe you can contact him?' She gives you the number. Beatrice says she cannot come to see Elaine just at present, because she lives 50 miles away, but says she will try to see her again soon.

You thank her very much and go back to see Elaine. By this time, Susan has found an old coat for her, and she is shivering less. She refuses to go back to her flat, but she lets you ring the on-call social worker, who says she will try to sort something out for her. You tell her that you have rung her sister, and although she cannot come at present, she will try to come soon. You say to her, 'Your sister says you were seeing a nurse called Danny. When did you last see him?'

She replies, 'Oh, I didn't like the injections. It's a few months since I've seen him.'

'Do you mind if I ring Danny tomorrow to ask if he will see you?'

She is happy with this. You also tell her that she should see her doctor. She agrees to do this, and fortunately Susan is free the following morning and arranges to accompany her.

What is likely to be the matter with this lady?

This lady may have schizophrenia. She has been struggling with the experience of hearing voices that call out to her. These voices tell her that people are going to harm her. Although she has been on medication, recently she has not been taking her monthly injections.

How can one help in this situation?

Firstly, it is raining and she has no coat. She needs a coat as well as food and drink and shelter. These are her immediate practical needs. Elaine also needs to be encouraged to go to see her doctor to make sure that she obtains appropriate medication. So, in a situation like this, there are several areas in which one can offer help. It is also necessary to try to find out who else is involved with her care.

What is schizophrenia?

Schizophrenia affects around one per cent of the population. The key difficulty in schizophrenia is the difficulty in separating 'real' and 'non-real' experiences. People with schizophrenia may believe that people are talking about them in a nasty way. There is often loss of concentration and withdrawal from work, family and friends. Frequently there is a change in personality. They may betray little emotion, interest and motivation. We often think of them as being very 'flat' emotionally. Sometimes there may be very little speech, and their thoughts at times seem inaccessible. People with schizophrenia may turn to drugs and alcohol for relief, which can compound their problems. Those with both schizophrenia and drug abuse or dependence can be very difficult to treat. With a whole host of newer drugs of abuse becoming available, this can make treatment even more complicated.

The thoughts of a person with schizophrenia might appear to jump around or to be slow. Thoughts can be experienced as disappearing completely or being replaced by another person's thoughts in their head. The person may appear confused and may find it difficult to make decisions. The individual may believe that the radio or television is talking about them, or that other people are in control of them in unusual ways. Elaine had the experience of hearing her neighbour, Bert, continually talking about her. These voices were very persistent and were occurring when Bert was nowhere in the vicinity. Recently these voices had been threatening, and Elaine had felt a need to leave her home even though it was raining heavily.

The ability to work and engage socially is usually affected in schizophrenia, although this is variable, depending on the stage of the illness and its severity. In Elaine's case, she had managed to get back to work for a brief period, but had since then been unable to work.

It is a lonely illness. Those who suffer from schizophrenia often find their existence is quite isolated, and they can feel very cut off from other people. Elaine is isolated. It is some months since she has seen her sister. The nature of her experiences and, in particular, her hearing the threatening voice of her neighbour, Bert, make it difficult for her to establish close links with her neighbours.

What is the outlook like for someone with schizophrenia?

Twenty per cent will recover; 60 per cent will get better but may have recurrences; 20 per cent will remain unwell for long periods.[1] Modern treatments do enable many more people to live reasonable lives outside hospital.

There is increasing evidence to suggest that the earlier in the illness the treatment is commenced, then the better the outcome.

I can remember as a medical student based in London, going to a psychiatric hospital in the countryside. The hospital was filled to bursting point with more than 1,000 patients. People in the corridors maintained strange and unusual postures. This situation thankfully no longer exists in the UK. With modern treatments, and treatment in the community, things have changed dramatically. Some, however, would argue that the pendulum has swung too far. In the old mental hospitals, people had the opportunity to do fairly basic types of work, and there was a degree of protection for them. Today, although community treatment is very helpful for many, some still 'fall through the gap' and can end up back in hospital, or in prison. Although we might talk about 'Care in the Community', the community can sometimes be an uncaring place! Someone like Elaine might be able to manage in the community with very careful supervision, if she continues to take her medication, but it is easy to see how things can go wrong and how she can become vulnerable.

Certainly, there are some patients who have really benefited from long-term hospital treatment and cannot successfully live in the community even though extensive care is available there. Yet, currently, with a restricted number of in-patient beds being available, care in hospital is also problematic. Often the acute hospital ward can be a very disturbed environment.

What else may people with schizophrenia be experiencing?

There may be false beliefs or delusions present. They may have strange beliefs about what is happening to them. They might believe that people are after them and want to harm them. Elaine was having these kinds of distressing experiences after she stopped taking her medication. Her beliefs about Bert were very fixed. They could not be shaken. These are delusions. Sometimes a delusion can actually be a true belief. However, the person believes the true thing for a completely wrong reason. For example, a woman might believe that her husband is having an affair because she perceives one night that the stars are shining particularly brightly. The reality might be that the husband *is* having an affair, but it is still a delusion because the belief is held for completely the wrong reason and has nothing whatever to do with the stars shining brightly!

The person with schizophrenia may well be having hallucinations, of which there are different kinds. The most typical is to hear voices that no one else can hear, and these voices seem to be coming from outside the person. They are being heard with the ears. Elaine was experiencing these voices fairly constantly, even when Bert was nowhere near. Sometimes these voices can tell the person to perform actions such as to harm themselves or other people. When they take on this 'command' nature they can be quite dangerous and will usually need rapid treatment. The hallucinations may not be auditory. A person may have a sensation that they are being touched. Sometimes the person may see things that are not actually present. (This kind of visual experience can also occur in delirium and other physical illnesses.) The person with schizophrenia may become withdrawn, with little speech and motivation.

What do we know about the causes of schizophrenia?

In mental illness in general we find that there is rarely one specific cause. Rather, there may be several factors that may make the condition more likely. For example, there is a genetic predisposition for most mental illness. However, what happens in the person's environment is also very important in the development of mental illness. Social situations and life events may contribute. Other illnesses and drugs may be factors.

Are genetic factors involved?

If one identical twin suffers from schizophrenia, the other twin has an almost 50 per cent chance of having schizophrenia. One might imagine the risk would be 100 per cent if the illness were purely genetically based. However, the risk is just 50 per cent. This indicates that although the genetic risk is considerable, there are other factors involved.[2]

The early environment is also important. With schizophrenia, we recognise that obstetric complications and possibly maternal viruses during pregnancy may affect the child. Often, those who later develop schizophrenia show evidence of slight delays in early development or social adjustment. Childhood deprivation and physical and sexual abuse increase the risk. Those who tend to be preoccupied in their own world or paranoid can be more at risk of schizophrenia.

What are the social factors involved in schizophrenia?

With schizophrenia, we recognise that it is more common in certain immigrant groups and in inner cities. The rate is higher in men. We recognise that people with schizophrenia, when they suffer criticism or over-involvement of others in their lives, can relapse as a result.

How may other illnesses or drugs influence the presentation of schizophrenia?

We recognise there is a connection between cannabis (particularly the stronger forms such as skunk) and schizophrenia. This has become much more evident over the last few years, with several key papers being written on this subject. There is also a risk of cocaine and amphetamines causing psychosis. Psychosis occurs when somebody is out of touch with reality and has difficulty separating real and unreal events.

Are there changes in the brain in schizophrenia?

There is evidence of slight shrinkage in brain tissue in chronic schizophrenia. Also, it seems that there is a disturbance in the way the different parts of the brain connect with each other. There is usually an alteration in brain chemistry. In the brain there are certain chemicals, termed neurotransmitters, that help nerve cells transmit messages to each other. Dopamine and glutamate are neurotransmitters whose function may be abnormal in schizophrenia.

Schizophrenia is also a complicated illness that may present in many different ways. Many psychiatrists these days consider it not to be just one illness, but rather prefer to talk about 'The Schizophrenias', recognising this diversity and complexity.

It is important to understand something of the range of possible factors and the ways these may interact, so that we do not think about mental illness in simplistic terms.

What else can we learn from Elaine's illness?

- Firstly, we can appreciate the need for drugs in treatment and can see how an illness can relapse when medication is not taken as prescribed.

- Secondly, we can see the need for careful follow-up for those with mental illness. If a person does not appear for an appointment, it may be necessary to make personal contact, if at all possible, to try to persuade them to accept help, so that relapse can be prevented.

- Thirdly, we can see the importance of different professions being involved. In Elaine's case, the key people were the doctors (both the psychiatrist and the general practitioner), the social worker and the community psychiatric nurse. In many situations the help of an occupational therapist will prove invaluable. CBT can also be helpful. It is important that there is good communication between the various professionals involved to ensure appropriate care for Elaine. Other professional support may also be needed, and vocational rehabilitation and recovery workers can help an individual look towards work and other possibilities in the future. Art and other therapies may prove valuable. Supported accommodation is often necessary. Also, the family is very important, and it was a pity that Elaine had refused contact with her sister following their disagreement.

- Finally, the importance of simple practical measures should not be forgotten. Ensuring that food, drink, warmth and clothing are provided can be very important. Those with schizophrenia tend to have poorer physical health than the general population, and may need help and encouragement with reducing smoking, taking exercise and having a proper diet. In mental illness we may not know the cause, and we may not have the cure, but we can still show that we care.

[1] Royal College of Psychiatrists 'Health Advice Leaflet, Schizophrenia,' www.rcpsych.ac.uk (accessed 03/09/2015).
[2] Ibid.

Recommended resources

Paranoid Thoughts (Institute of Psychiatry website to help people with unfounded or excessive fears about others): www.paranoidthoughts.com (accessed 4th September 2015).

Rethink Mental Illness (information support and help for people affected by mental illness): www.rethink.org (accessed 4th September 2015).

Mind (Information and help on all aspects of mental health): www.mind.org.uk (accessed 4th September 2015).

Chapter ten
Spiritual help in schizophrenia

Loneliness, as we have mentioned, is common amongst those with schizophrenia. They may find it difficult to trust others, and with the difficulties they have in separating real and non-real experiences, they can find the world a confusing place. They may find it difficult to engage socially. How can the church or concerned individuals support and encourage them?

There are many ways we can do this. Encouraging them to maintain family connections and friendships as well as involvement in group activities is often necessary. Guiding them to develop wider interests can be important. Helping them, where possible, to give of themselves, and engage, for example, in voluntary activity can be beneficial.

The church should be accepting of people with mental health issues and help them integrate. An interesting development here, called Person Centred Churches, was initiated by hospital chaplain Peter Richmond. [1] He understood the difficulties people with mental illness might have in integrating into some churches. His desire was to make churches more friendly and person centred for those with disabilities and mental illness.

There are other ways the church can help. Having a warm and friendly drop-in centre, where people can come for coffee and just enjoy being there, can be valuable for many who might be struggling with mental illness. Having simple activities and games available can be an asset. A drop-in club or meeting place may be able to offer help with debt relief and financial problems (Christians Against Poverty[2] [CAP] is very good at this). Providing links to enable people to engage in simple employment and voluntary opportunities can be useful. Assisting people to fill out difficult and complicated forms could help them take a step forward into employment.

The more we understand the illness, the better we will be able to identify with the person. We will realise, for example in schizophrenia, that to be too demanding or critical might prove unhelpful. We might be able to help provide support for the carers of those with mental illness. One interesting initiative here was taken by Janet Love whose son developed psychosis whilst she was training to become a psychotherapist. She began an organisation called Loving Someone in Psychosis – Help us, Help our Loved ones.[3] This aims to encourage the development of self-help networks to support the families and friends of those who have developed psychosis.

It is very easy for the main carers to become burnt out with the strain, and we will want to try to help with this. It might mean, for example, providing the carer with some space and time, while the person with mental health problems attends a church drop-in club. We also need to recognise our limits. We cannot do everything, nor should we try. It is important to have good connections with health and social services and work in collaboration with them.

As Christians, we believe in the power of prayer. This prayer needs to be sensitive. For example, it can be either with the individual or for the individual, depending on the circumstances. Sometimes, in the more acute situation, one is happy to pray *for* the person, rather than *with* the person. We need to be aware that the person may be vulnerable and we must never be in the position of seeking to force our opinions or views upon them. Also, it is helpful for clergy and Christian leaders to liaise with psychiatrists and other professionals in seeking to provide as well-rounded care as possible.

We can encourage people in the Christian faith. We may be able to encourage them to believe that they are valued and loved. They may have been treated badly or rejected by others, so forgiveness may be an issue. We can remind them of the forgiveness that is available through Christ. We want to encourage them that despite their difficulties, they have a role in life, and we want to help them find it. Also, we may remind them that they belong to a wider body – the church – that can provide help for them. We need to apply these truths to their lives with sensitivity.

Mental illness and demon possession?

One of the questions I am asked when I am giving talks on mental health issues is this: 'Can you explain demon possession, and is demon possession related to mental illness?' This question is often asked when I am discussing schizophrenia, perhaps because most people find this the most difficult of the mental illnesses to understand.

There are two Bible passages that can help us to think about this question. The first one comes from the prophecy of Daniel and relates to the illness of King Nebuchadnezzar:

> [H]e [King Nebuchadnezzar] said, 'Is not this the great Babylon I have built as the royal residence, by my mighty power and for the glory of my majesty?'
>
> Even as the words were on his lips, a voice came from heaven, 'This is what is decreed for you, King Nebuchadnezzar: Your royal authority has been taken from you. You will be driven away from people and will live with the wild animals; you will eat grass like the ox. Seven times will pass by for you until you acknowledge that the Most High is sovereign over all kingdoms on earth and gives them to anyone he wishes.'
>
> Immediately what had been said about Nebuchadnezzar was fulfilled. He was driven away from people and ate grass like the ox. His body was drenched with the dew of heaven until his hair grew like the feathers of an eagle and his nails like the claws of a bird.
>
> At the end of that time, I, Nebuchadnezzar, raised my eyes towards heaven, and my sanity was restored. Then I praised the Most High; I honoured and glorified him who lives for ever.
>
> *Daniel 4:30–34a*

Here we have the mighty king, Nebuchadnezzar, being humbled by God on account of his pride. Following this pride, there was a period of seven years during which he became very disturbed. Daniel describes him as leaving the company of men and going out into the fields and eating grass like a wild animal. He allowed his nails to grow into claws. He lost his sanity and then regained it after seven years. There is no indication here of demonic forces at work, but there seems to be mental illness and recovery from it. In this process, King Nebuchadnezzar learned something about the true God and began to worship Him.

On turning our attention to look at demonic forces, we see that Jesus Christ and His disciples were frequently involved in the casting out of demons. Here is one example where Jesus confronts a demon-possessed man:

> When he saw Jesus from a distance, he ran and fell on his knees in front of him. He shouted at the top of his voice, 'What do you want with me, Jesus, Son of the Most High God? In God's name don't torture me!'
> *Mark 5:6–7*

Jesus casts the demons out of the man, and He allows the demons, of which there were very many, to go into a herd of 2,000 pigs, which rushed over a cliff and were drowned. The man was healed. The surrounding villagers, instead of rejoicing over the man who was healed, asked Jesus to leave their area.

Here it is interesting to note the difference from the story of King Nebuchadnezzar. Unlike the previous account, there is clear evidence of the presence of demons. The demons felt tortured by the presence and authority of Jesus Christ. They cried out when they encountered His presence, because they knew that they had to obey the voice of Jesus Christ and come out of the man.

Many churches make mistakes and cause damage by attributing mental illness to demonic forces. Recently, whilst abroad, a church leader asked for my advice on a particular situation regarding a man in his congregation. He mentioned that several people had been trying to drive out demons from him, but without success. Now the man had begun to withdraw from church and seemed unhappy, as others in the church were treating him differently because they believed he was demon-possessed. When it was discussed with me, it appeared quite clear that the person involved was suffering from schizophrenia and had been hurt, rather than helped, by unsuccessful attempts to drive out demons. He needed gentle restoration and understanding.

However, demon possession is not unknown today. The leader of another church abroad was faced with the following situation. He had noticed that a girl in his congregation seemed to be suffering from demon possession and invited her and her friend for special prayer. (Demonic possession may be noted at times in a Christian meeting, where Christ is proclaimed and the presence of God is experienced by the worshippers. It can lead to a person who is possessed behaving strangely, with shrieking, writhing or similar manifestations in this setting.) He observed that the girl was writhing around on the floor and desperately trying to cover her ears when the name of Jesus Christ was mentioned. There was a definite connection between the name of Christ and the demonic manifestations. As the name of Christ was mentioned the manifestations increased very obviously, with writhing and gross discomfort, loud noises and attempts to cover the ears, so that the girl could not hear the name of Jesus Christ. After a while, proceedings were halted, and the simple truths of the gospel and salvation through Christ were explained to the girl concerned. She was aware enough and willing to receive Christ into her life.

Following this, and a time of praise and worship in Jesus' name, the demons caused no further trouble, and the girl left in a much calmer and more relaxed frame of mind.

Demon possession is a reality, although it is usually very different in nature from classic mental illness.

Summary of chapters nine and ten

- Understanding schizophrenia helps us to identify with the person who is suffering.

- Practical care and inclusion for the person can be very important.

- Medication and good liaison between caring professionals is vital.

- The church can set an example of love and care by including and helping those with schizophrenia and their carers.

- Demon possession is a reality, although it is usually very different in nature from classic mental illness.

[1] Person Centred Churches, East Kent NHS and Social Care Partnership Trust, St. Martin's Hospital, Littlebourne Road, Canterbury CT1 1TD (Tel 01227 812047) (ASPCC Resource Pack on Spiritual and Mental Health www.mentalhealthmatters-cofe.org Accessed 05/10/2015).

[2] Christians Against Poverty (CAP) www.capuk.org (accessed 5th October 2015).

[3] Loving Someone in Psychosis – Help us, help our Loved Ones, 7 Moon Street, London N1 0QU (ASPCC Resource Pack on Spiritual and Mental Health www.mentalhealthmatters-cofe.org (accessed 5th October 2015).

Chapter eleven
The person with dementia

> Pray, do not mock me:
> I am a very foolish fond old man,
> Fourscore and upward, not an hour more nor
> less;
> And, to deal plainly,
> I fear I am not in my perfect mind.
> Methinks I should know you, and know this man;
> Yet I am doubtful for I am mainly ignorant
> What place this is; and all the skill I have
> Remembers not these garments; nor I know not
> Where I did lodge last night. Do not laugh at me;
> For, as I am a man, I think this lady
> To be my child Cordelia.
> (William Shakespeare, *King Lear*, Act 4, Scene
> VII)

King Lear here has difficulty remembering what he has been doing recently. He thinks he is not in his perfect mind. He struggles to remember where he is, and does not recognise his own clothing. He then thinks he remembers his own daughter, but is not fully sure.

Many people have problems with their memory as they grow older, whereas others remain mentally sharp, well into great old age.

Problems with memory may begin insidiously, and in some people it remains a simple memory problem. With others, there is progressive memory decline, accompanied by loss of abilities.

Imagine the following scenario.

You have been happily married to your husband, George, for 45 years, and then you notice that he is beginning to have problems with his memory. You consult your family doctor, and he refers you to a psychiatrist for the elderly to whom you are relating the recent difficulties.

You tell him, 'Well, doctor, it started with his memory about six months ago. He asked me about the arrangements for our summer holiday three times in the space of an hour. He then forgot an important arrangement to meet a friend in town. He started to misplace things. He lost his car keys, and we found them in the fridge. He was very upset about that and started shouting at me and accusing me of taking them. That kind of behaviour is most unusual for George. Then on one occasion he drove the wrong way down a one-way street and could not understand why all the other drivers were honking at him. He has scraped the car quite badly on a couple of occasions recently. He has been forgetting to take his medication, and the other day he tried to give the window cleaner £100 for cleaning the windows. He cannot now seem to use his bank card and the other day put in the wrong pin code on three occasions. He also seems to have difficulty using the remote control for the television. His memory just seems to be getting worse and worse.'

The psychiatrist assesses him carefully. George is not able to give a very accurate account of himself, seems not to be able to remember exactly how long he has been married, and gets very confused when asked the ages of his children. The doctor performs a memory test, and George scores 22 out of a possible 30 points. He then asks George to put the numbers around a clock face, and put the hands on the clock to make the time ten past eleven. George puts the numbers all down one side of the clock and then points one hand towards the number 11 and the other towards the number ten. He asks George to identify and count some coins for him, and George insists that the 10p coin is a shilling and the 5p coin is sixpence (this was the previous coinage system in the UK). He is unable to count the coins.

The psychiatrist then begins to explain things to both of you carefully. He says that George has a condition called dementia. He explains that this has affected George's memory and his abilities. George gets very upset when his driving is discussed. He says, 'I am a very good driver, doctor, and I have never had a problem all the time I have been driving.'

The doctor gently reminds George of the recent problems there have been. In the end, George reluctantly agrees to stop driving. You then discuss the problems George has in managing his finances. The doctor mentions the possibilities of arranging a Power of Attorney, but in discussion you simply agree to manage the finances from now on. You also agree to manage George's medications. The psychiatrist advises you about a tablet that might help George's memory, called Aricept. He explains that the tablet will not cure the dementia, but it may well help to hold it back for a year or two. He also offers the opportunity of a home visit by a member of the team working with the elderly so you can have a fuller explanation of everything that has been discussed, and to make sure that further help can be given as needed.

This was all about two years ago. It was quite difficult initially to dissuade George from driving, and you found you needed considerable patience in persuading George to pass over his bank cards and cheque books which he had begun to use unwisely and inaccurately. A scan showed some slight shrinkage of the brain. The

Aricept, for the first year or so, certainly seemed to help. Now, though, things seem to be getting worse again. George's personal hygiene is not quite as good as before. You need to encourage him to shower and change his clothing. His memory is getting gradually worse. He begins to be incontinent of urine. He makes mistakes sometimes whilst dressing. The other day he put his pyjama bottoms on over his trousers.

On holiday three months ago in a hotel in Portugal he could not seem to find his way back to the room one night. You observe now that in new surroundings he has difficulty in finding his way. You become worried that if he went outside alone, he might become lost.

Dementia is a serious illness, more present in the elderly than in those who are younger. To make a confident diagnosis, there needs to be at least six months' evidence of deterioration in memory and abilities. There is often also a change in personality.

George, who had always been a quiet man, began to have angry outbursts. Now you find that these have been getting worse. The other day he began to swear in the local shop because they did not have the chocolates he wanted. You were very embarrassed and tried to explain that he was not well, before hurrying out of the shop. Judging from the face of the shop assistant, you are not sure that you will be going back to that shop again!

What are the various kinds of dementia?

The most common type is named Alzheimer's disease, after Alois Alzheimer who, in 1901, initially described the condition in a woman of 50. This lady gradually showed memory and then mental and physical decline. Although it can occur in younger people, as Alzheimer described, it is more commonly a disease of the elderly.

There are other kinds of dementia apart from Alzheimer's disease. Sometimes a person will have a dementia following a major stroke or several minor strokes. This is termed vascular dementia, and about 20 per cent of dementia can be vascular in type. In Lewy body dementia there are often visual hallucinations of people or animals, varying confusion during the day and trembling, stiffness and falls. There are memory difficulties and problems in planning tasks. Another variety of dementia is called frontotemporal dementia. This often affects rather younger people. They may present with bizarre behaviour and a loss of social awareness. They may act in sexually inappropriate ways, or appear rude in social situations. Their speech may be affected quite early on, and they can tend to experience difficulty finding names for things, or their speech may become fragmented. Sometimes they may appear withdrawn and apathetic.

Can dementia be found in other situations?

Those who have Down's syndrome often develop dementia in later life. Those with Parkinson's disease, AIDS and other conditions can develop dementia. Sometimes the blood tests carried out by the local doctor point to a cause of dementia which is treatable, such as can occasionally happen with a vitamin deficiency or hormonal imbalance. Dementia can be a result of very heavy alcohol intake, and abstinence can sometimes be followed by a degree of improvement. There are also several quite rare forms of dementia.

Dementia needs to be carefully distinguished from two other conditions which are quite common in the elderly. Firstly, dementia needs to be distinguished from an acute confusional state, or delirium. We have mentioned that in dementia there is at least a six-month period of gradually increasing loss of memory, together with loss of abilities in some areas and often a change in personality. There are many causes, however, of acute confusion of short duration. Chest or urinary or other infections can cause this. Changes in medication or being in hospital in a strange environment can lead to acute confusion, particularly in the elderly, and there are many other contributory factors. In these cases, the doctor investigates and treats the causes that have led to the confusion.

Secondly, a person with depression may seem confused. They may seem to have dementia. This has often been called a pseudo-dementia. However, in these cases, if the depression is identified and treated, then the confusion will often clear.

How common is dementia?

It is increasingly common with advancing age. For example, one in 14 aged 65 and over, and one in six over the age of 80, have dementia. Currently in the UK there are around 850,000 patients with dementia, and the number is increasing.[1] Around one-third of people with dementia live by themselves.[2]

How can we help the person with dementia, and their carers?

Let us go back to the case of George, being looked after by his wife, Mary, who recounts the following:

After the initial assessment, things went fairly well for a year or 18 months, but I then found I needed more help. I had to watch George all the time. I was also worried when he wanted to go out. I felt I always had to go with him for his own safety. Nights also were becoming difficult. One night I was embarrassed by the police knocking on the door, and waking me up, to ask me if this man dressed only in his pyjamas was my husband. Apparently he had been wandering in the road a couple of streets away, and a neighbour had called the police. I became quite exhausted. Now, fortunately, he is attending a local day centre two days a week. I have needed to make one or two changes to the home, and we now have new bathroom facilities on the ground floor. Although George is walking quite well, he can be a little unsteady, and the occupational therapist came round and arranged an extra handrail for the stairs, which are quite steep.

And then I had a small stroke and could not move so well. Also George in his nightly visits to the bathroom was getting so disorientated that sometimes he was wetting the carpet in the bedroom next door by mistake. And then, when he had a urinary tract infection, he became much more confused. Eventually, despite wanting George to remain at home, I felt I could cope no longer, and with advice from the social worker, I decided I would look at possible residential facilities. Initially we decided to try one for a couple of weeks while I went to visit my sister who lives in Cornwall. I needed a break and Michael, our son, said he would be happy to keep an eye on George.

Well, I was surprised how well this worked for George. My holiday went well and George was quite happy in the home after the first day or so. In the future, we might see if this residential home is suitable for George, if I find I cannot manage things at home.

I can really commend this home. There is a pleasant atmosphere about it. There is a range of activities available for residents. The staff relate to those with dementia as people rather than just as dementia cases – if you understand my meaning. I noticed that when they admitted George, they spent time finding out about him in detail. I told them that he had been a plumber and really enjoyed football. They asked me if they could put up a board by his bed with these details on it, to help staff engage in conversation with him. They made a very good job of this board, and George had some excellent chats with various members of staff.

I heard, through the grapevine, that the home down the road is a very different place. There the old people are left around the edge of the room, with the television blaring in the corner. No one talks to each other, and the staff don't seem to have a clue about the life stories of the individual residents. I heard of a man who was very ill recently, having been given a large dose of sedatives. It seems he had become a bit aggressive. It later transpired, however, on more careful review, that he had a weak bladder and might just have been trying to find the toilet.

How can we understand behavioural problems in dementia?

People with dementia frequently develop problems in their behaviour which can be difficult to understand and manage. They often have difficulty in communicating their needs and wishes. There may be personal neglect. There may be problems with socially inappropriate behaviour; this can be troublesome within the home and also in public places. There can be restlessness present, and a tendency to wander without fully understanding where they are going.

George showed this when he went out for a walk at night, clad only in his pyjamas. Physical aggression can sometimes occur, although this is less common than verbal outbursts.

With all types of behaviour, it is important to try to understand what the person is communicating by their behaviour. For example, someone might have an urgent need to visit the toilet, but be unable to find it, and might become aggressive if this need is not understood. Sedative medication may be given inappropriately and this can have serious effects on mobility and general well-being.

On other occasions, certain behaviour can be understood in the light of previous patterns of activity before admission to a care environment. For example, someone may, before retiring to bed, have gone round to check the doors and windows every night to ensure everything was safe before retiring. This same checking behaviour might recur in the residential facility. An understanding of previous routines will help here, and perhaps the individual could even be given a set of false keys to use at night.

As well as understanding difficult behaviour and trying to work out its causes, there are ways of providing a calm and less stressful environment. Music can be very valuable. Aromatherapy, using lavender or similar oils, can help calm someone who might be quite disturbed. (Caution is needed, however, since some New Age practitioners may attribute their healing properties to 'balancing energy flows' within the body.) Provision of a soothing environment can be very necessary. Pets can be therapeutic, and it is interesting to see the reaction and interest aroused when a dog is introduced into a circle of elderly people.

What drug treatments are available for dementia?

Medication is now available to help those with the Alzheimer's type of dementia, and it is also often useful in Lewy body dementia. Medication is not curative, but may delay progression of the illness over a one- to two-year period. This may well help a person to remain in their home for a longer period of time and with an improved quality of life. One of the drugs that is given is Aricept and there are other alternatives. Between 40 and 70 per cent of people are helped by the drug, but some may not respond. Drugs such as this one increase the level of a substance in the brain called acetylcholine. It is believed that an increased level of this substance (which acts as a neurotransmitter, enabling nerve cells to communicate) helps to slow down the deterioration in the memory.

Another drug that is sometimes used in dementia is called Ebixa or Memantine. This acts in a slightly different way in the middle and later stages of dementia and can help memory and reduce agitation and aggression.

In vascular dementia, small doses of aspirin to help prevent strokes can be valuable, and treatment for high blood pressure and raised cholesterol may be needed.

Some drugs are best avoided in dementia since they can make the person worse. Occasionally, there can be a need to prescribe a tablet to help people sleep, but ideally this should be for short-term rather than for prolonged usage.

It is best to avoid sedatives and sleeping tablets, since they can cause excessive sedation, and then a person could get up during the night and possibly fall.

What about the genetics of dementia?

In very rare instances, people may develop a dementia in their forties and early fifties; this type of dementia tends to run in particular families. Also, in the elderly population some families are rather more likely to develop dementia than others. There are certain proteins that are more associated with dementia. One of these is called apolipoprotein E. This protein exists in different forms, and depending on the exact form present, dementia can be more or less likely.

What other substances can help the person with dementia?

Other substances are sometimes used to complement drugs. For example, some people recommend ginkgo biloba, but its benefit is very doubtful. Vitamin B12 and folate can be necessary where there is a deficiency of these substances. Some believe that fish oils containing omega-3 fatty acids can be valuable. There is no evidence of any vaccination that can currently help dementia.

What can increase the risk of dementia?

Smoking, obesity, excess alcohol, diabetes, raised cholesterol and high blood pressure can all increase the risk.

What conditions can be confused with dementia?

Sometimes a person does not have a true dementia, but simply has difficulty with their memory. The memory is not as good as it might be, but the person is still able to function absolutely normally. Learning to take notes and posting personal reminders often helps these individuals. Keeping the mind active by reading, crossword puzzles and the like can be important. Physical exercise is generally beneficial. These people may be referred to as having 'mild cognitive impairment'. In about 50 per cent of these cases the person will eventually develop dementia. However, this then means that 50 per cent do not develop dementia and, indeed, can sometimes improve. At times, an individual with severe anxiety may be concerned about their memory and the possibility of dementia, but they can usually be reassured following careful assessment.

What principles should guide the care of a person with dementia?

It is important that care is person centred. Use of language often betrays our thoughts regarding a person. We can say, 'This is a *demented* person,' or we can say, 'This is a *person*

197

who has dementia.' It is important that we meet the person as a real individual. This 'meeting' of a real person is vital in identifying with and helping that individual. Martin Buber, the Austrian-born Jewish philosopher, said, 'All real living is meeting.'[3] He was emphasising the importance of truly relating to a person. Really meeting with the person, despite the presence of the dementia, is very important.

If the main focus is on someone like George, above, then it is important to find out as much about George as possible, as this will help us to care appropriately. Looking at his life history can be very important. For example, what was his occupation? What were his main beliefs and interests? What about his family life and relationships?

Good practice would be to construct a board to go in George's room (with the consent of George and his family) detailing the major aspects of his life, as an aid for staff and visitors to engage with him. In George's case, this board really helped staff communicate well with him. It is important that all staff understand and adhere to the principles of person-centred care. This happened in the home to which George was admitted.

How else can we help the person with more severe dementia in a residential or nursing placement?

Engaging someone in group activities can be very valuable. It is important that someone like George is not just put to the periphery of a large 'day room' with a television blaring loudly in the corner, with most people paying little attention to it, or to each other. It is much better to try to engage George in activities of some description and to give him individual attention. We need to pay particular regard to the relationships and needs of someone like George. One very helpful book here is Tom Kitwood's *Dementia Reconsidered*.[4]

What are the main psychosocial needs of someone with dementia?

Essentially, these can be grouped around the principle of truly loving and caring for them. There are five key needs that a person like George has:

- Firstly, a sense of attachment.

- Secondly, a sense of belonging.

- Thirdly, a sense of comfort.

- Fourthly, a sense of identity, which implies that the person will feel included, and their opinions are valued.

- Fifthly, there will be occupation.

In the nursing home environment, it is important that someone like George feels comfortable and at home. Sometimes people are seen as objects rather than as real people with dementia. Occupation can often be with simple tasks. For example, a previous housewife could be given opportunities to carry out simple tasks such as folding laundry. A gentleman who used to like dismantling things could be given old radios to work with.

Reminiscence therapy involving the talking through of past experiences and events can prove helpful. Spiritual needs are also important. What are George's beliefs, and does he have the opportunity, or can he be helped, to express his beliefs in a meaningful way?

To what extent can people with dementia make their own decisions?

A person like George should be given the opportunity to engage in decisions about care and support wherever possible. Sometimes a person may not have the level of insight necessary, and decisions may need to be taken for the person, for their safety. For example, someone might not be able to decide whether they can live safely at home, because of lack of insight into the risks involved. However, even in this situation, it is usually better to manage the risks in the home environment for as long as possible, rather than move someone like George too readily to a residential or nursing environment. Sometimes a person may be able to live at home throughout the illness. This will depend a lot on family commitment, the strain on the family, and the ability, in various ways, to provide appropriate care for someone like George at home. However, if insight is lacking and a person is incapable of making a decision to stay safely at home, it does not mean that all decisions are taken away from the person. A person like George may not be able to manage his own finances, but can well decide what he wants from the lunch menu! It is a common mistake to assume that because George cannot make one particular decision, he cannot make any decisions at all.

What about the needs of those who are caring for people with dementia?

It is important for someone like Mary, above, to find help and support to cope with what can be a very demanding and lonely role. Carers need to have daily time for themselves. Mary should be enabled, if she wishes, to find time to get out of the home, without George, at least on a weekly basis, and preferably more frequently. This might be to play golf or visit the hairdresser, for example. It is also important for Mary to be able to plan an occasional weekend away.

For this to happen, there may need to be an increase in support for George during this time, either from the family, or through increased statutory service provision. Care in a day centre can be very helpful, or respite care in a nursing or residential home may be necessary. It is important that someone like Mary gets sufficient sleep, and sometimes a night-time sitting rota can be arranged. Mary may need help and encouragement to pay attention to her own needs, such as maintaining a reasonable diet and taking regular exercise.

It is well known that carers can become depressed, or anxious and stressed. Mary might need encouragement to book an appointment to see her local doctor if this happens to her. Sometimes carers can request flexible working hours because of their home responsibilities. It needs to be ensured that Mary gets help with understanding and managing George's behavioural problems.

It is important that if Mary gets fatigued, she can find help with this. If she finds appropriate help (and this may not always be easy), then she may well be enabled to cope for longer in this difficult role. Sometimes carers need encouragement to continue with important personal relationships. There can be a tendency for other people to withdraw when faced with an illness such as dementia in a relative or friend. This can prove quite painful, particularly for someone like Mary. Often the carer may not understand the illness and may benefit from a careful explanation. This can be given by a member of the team. Also, the Alzheimer's Society can be very helpful in this regard. Someone like Mary may need to draw up contingency plans if she becomes ill. In this situation, extra support may well be needed. Mary may need extra practical help with skills such as lifting or maybe transport, as she is unable to drive. There is a national dementia helpline available through the Alzheimer's Society.[5]

[1] Dementia UK 2014 Demography, Alzheimer's Society: www.alzheimers.org.uk (accessed 3rd September 2015).
[2] 'People with dementia living alone', Alzheimer's Society: www.alzheimers.org.uk (accessed 3rd September 2015).
[3] Martin Buber, *I and Thou* (New York, Scribner, 1958), pp. 24–25.
[4] Oxford University Press, 1997.
[5] Alzheimer's Society helpline: 0300 222 1122 (as of 3rd September 2015).

Recommended resources

Tom Kitwood, *Dementia Reconsidered* (Maidenhead, Oxford University Press, 1997).

Alzheimer's Society (research, advice and help on all aspects of dementia): www.alzheimers.org.uk (accessed 04/09/2015).

Age UK (advice and help on issues affecting older people): www.ageuk.org.uk (accessed 04/09/2015).

Carers UK (helping make life better for carers): www.carersuk.org (accessed 04/09/2015).

The Lewy Body Society (promoting awareness and research in Lewy body dementia): www.lewybody.org (accessed 4th September 2015).

The Law Society (provides useful legal information on such issues of making a Power of Attorney and other arrangements): www.lawsociety.org.uk (accessed 4th September 2015).

Chapter twelve
Spiritual help in dementia

One of the questions I have been asked in my clinic is, 'Why me?' What might lie behind this question? Let us take an example. A person has a spouse with dementia and is struggling with the burden of care. The spouse has changed and is not the same person that they married. There might be behavioural change and the spouse might be verbally aggressive, as happened with George. Someone like Mary, above, may find it difficult to relate to George since they can no longer enjoy a good conversation together. Mary might feel lonely and isolated as a result.

Mary might then begin to ask herself the question, 'Why must I care for George, who has changed so much?' The desire is often to keep someone like George at home. Mary feels an obligation to do what is best for him. However, the burden is often considerable, and a carer might feel abandoned. Families may help alleviate the burden, and also social services' care arrangements can help. However, the carer is still left with the person for most of the time. Incessant demands and repeated questions can be very wearing, as can difficult behaviour and aggressive tendencies. There may be an increased risk of someone like

George wandering or doing strange things in the home, leaving Mary with anxiety and considerable stress. Mary will also almost certainly struggle with the grief of losing the person she has known and loved, as George's illness progresses.

The illness shows a persistent downhill course. Medication may help for a while, but in the end there is always a progressive decline which may last for many years, unless some other terminal condition supervenes. The illness may progress over a period of seven to ten years, or even longer.

How can we understand severe continuing illness and still believe in a God of love? One way to do this is to look carefully at the understanding which the Bible gives us. The picture that we are given of the world is that it was created with beauty and harmony by a God who loved His creation and said that it was very good (Genesis 1:31). Humankind, however, turned away from God's commandment and sin entered this perfect world. Following this disobedience we read of pain, suffering and death. We also read of conflict, hard labour and a curse upon the ground (Genesis 3:14–19). The apostle Paul talks about this, describing a creation that is full of groaning, frustration and decay. He adds that we, too, in these bodies of ours, also groan. He sees, however, a coming day when all of this will radically change (Romans 8:19–24).

What we can say about this world we live in is that it does not have the same pristine beauty with which it was created, nor does it have the same beauty which it will have when Christ returns to reign. Since the Fall, as described in Genesis, suffering has been present in the world. This may show itself in mental or physical illness which may affect us at some stage, while deterioration will happen in all of our bodies. The world remains a place of toil, pain and death. This long-term suffering may be seen in the severe illnesses we encounter, and particularly, perhaps, in the case of dementia.

It is into this world of suffering and pain that Jesus came. We see Him bringing healing and blessing into all the lives He touched. Yet at the same time He goes forward to death at His Father's command. 'The reason my Father loves me is that I lay down my life – only to take it up again' (John 10:17). Christ Himself endured immense pain and suffering in His journey to the cross and on the cross itself. He is thus able to be a source of inspiration and strength to all who suffer and are in pain. The Bible also records, 'Surely he took up our pain and bore our suffering' (Isaiah 53:4). He identifies with us in all our pains and struggles since He has endured them to an even greater degree.

He brought healing to this world, when He lived on earth, and now that He has risen from the dead and is alive, this healing power can still be known today. We may not see the fullness of Christ's power in the healing of dementia, but particularly in places where the church is strong and united, remarkable miracles still occur. We also believe that Christ will return, and this will be a time when all things will be made perfectly new. We will even have new bodies to replace those that are broken now by pain, suffering and death. We eagerly await this coming day.

Until that day, we are called to love and care. Paul again writes, 'serve one another humbly in love' (Galatians 5:13) and, 'Carry each other's burdens, and in this way you will fulfil the law of Christ' (Galatians 6:2).

Each of us is made in the image of God and is of incomparable value. The supreme calling on our lives is to love and care for each other. There are so many ways this can be expressed towards those with dementia and their carers.

We can seek to ensure that those with dementia are well cared for, wherever they might reside. We can seek to drive up standards of care. We can find ways to identify with and include those with dementia wherever possible. We can try to ensure that those with dementia are treated with respect and as real individuals, despite their difficulties. We can seek to understand what might lie behind difficult behaviour patterns. We may need to slow down in our communication with them and may need to use simpler language. We can pray for them and with them, where appropriate. Even though they may not remember our visits, we can bring comfort and strength by our presence. We can encourage continued church involvement where desired, and we can encourage the local church community to remain interested and involved with them. (This is not always easy, as church congregations change or people move away, and the illness may gradually progress over many years.)

We can care for the carers by keeping in touch with them and supporting them emotionally and in many practical ways. We might be able to arrange a short break for the carer. We can link in with the Alzheimer's Society and other charities to help with information and care provision.

If we are people committed to serving in love, there will never be a shortage of opportunities.

The author Robert Louis Stevenson was very affected by the work of Father Damien, who looked after a colony of those who had leprosy on the island of Molokai in the West Indies. Father Damien contracted leprosy himself, and died from the same illness as those he went to care for. Stevenson visited Molokai shortly after Father Damien's death and found:

> ...abominable deformations of our common manhood ... a population as only now and then surrounds us in the horror of a nightmare ... the butt-ends of human beings lying there almost unrecognizable but still breathing, still thinking, still remembering ... a pitiful place to visit, a hell to dwell in.

Stevenson became friendly with those who worked on the island, and mixed freely with the lepers, and played with the children. At this stage, Stevenson himself was suffering from tuberculosis. What he saw on the island made a dramatic impact on him. Before leaving the island, Stevenson composed a poem giving his impression of the nuns who worked with the lepers. This was addressed to the Reverend Sister Marianne:

> Matron of the Bishop Home, Kalaupapa.
> To see the infinite pity of this place,
> The mangled limb, the devastated face,
> The innocent sufferers smiling at the rod,
> A fool were tempted to deny his God.

He sees, and shrinks; but if he look again,
Lo, beauty springing from the breasts of pain!
He marks the sisters on the painful shores,
And even a fool is silent and adores.[1] [2]

The story of Father Damien shows that love is prepared to make the ultimate sacrifice. Love brings tremendous power to change the lot of one's fellow human beings. Stevenson's reaction is interesting. At first he is so overpowered by the suffering that he is tempted to write God off as the perpetrator of some monstrous calamity. Later, as he reflects on the compassion shown by the nuns, he sees a greater power at work and that is the power of love. There is something greater than suffering, and that is love itself. Christ Himself shows this love by making the ultimate sacrifice and laying down His life for us. Through His sacrifice there flows the power for our lives and those around us to be changed.

Today, there is suffering and pain that impacts our lives in different ways. However, there is also the love and mercy shown by Christians through the Holy Spirit.

Whenever we look at the ministry of Christ, we never see Him causing pain and suffering to individuals; He is always bringing love and mercy to them. In the same way He has chosen the church as His instrument to bring love and mercy into the world.

Summary of chapters eleven and twelve

- Dementia is a progressive illness affecting, generally, the elderly.

- Treatment and help are available, but treatment is rarely curative.

- Person-centred care and maintenance of a person's dignity are always important.

- Carers need special help and consideration.

- Real love for the person, whatever their condition, must always be the guiding principle of our lives.

---

[1] Robert Louis Stevenson, *Father Damien: An Open Letter to the Reverend Dr Hyde of Honolulu*, 25th February 1890 (London: Chatto and Windus, 1914).

[2] From Fr F. E. Burns, 'The Strange Case of Father Damien and Robert Louis Stevenson'
www.ad2000.com.au/articles/2002/sep2002p10_1117.html
(accessed 3rd September 2015).

Conclusion
Faith and mental health problems

How may the Christian faith help us to understand and face mental health issues?

There are many ways, but I have selected six that I believe are of fundamental importance.

- First of all, many people with mental health problems do not know or feel that they have any value. Their self-esteem is often at rock bottom. They do not sense that they have any intrinsic value. In India there are people called the Dalits, or untouchables. In the Hindu faith, people are believed to be connected in some way to different parts of the Hindu god. For example, the uppermost Brahman caste is reputed to come from the head of the god. Likewise, the lesser castes come from different parts of the god. However, the Dalits are seen as coming from under the feet of the god and so do not belong. There are more than 250 million Dalits in India who 'do not belong' in this sense, and they are despised. They are given the most menial and loathsome jobs. For example, they may be rat catchers

211

or dung removers. These people previously had little sense of their own personal value. However, many of them have now opened the Bible and have found on the very first page these words: 'So God created mankind in his own image, in the image of God he created them; male and female he created them' (Genesis 1:27). The Dalits quickly realised that these words meant that every human being has been made by God and, instead of not belonging, they can now belong through the God of the Bible. They are important. They are wanted. In the Christian faith they are important to God, for they were made by Him. This has had a major effect on much of the Dalit population, and many have turned to faith in Christ, because they can see that in the Christian faith, each person has meaning and value.

However, although since the start of the century many have turned to the Christian faith (and many also to Buddhism), this has not necessarily removed discrimination against them, and in many cases they are actually worse off, with the loss of privileges afforded to Hindu Dalits over recent years. A few years ago I enjoyed helping out on a medical team serving the Dalits near Hyderabad in India. The team visited a school that had been provided for Dalit children. Although permitted to attend normal schools, they often feel ostracised by their peers and may drop out. The Good Shepherd schools[1] that have been set up recently, and the campaign for justice for the Dalits led by Joseph D'Souza [2] and others, are wonderful initiatives, although the general needs of the Dalits remain vast. As many Dalits have found a new sense of value through the knowledge that they are made in the image of God, in a similar way those with mental illness need to understand that they, too, are supremely valued.

- The second area where the Christian faith impacts mental illness is that people can know that they are loved. One of the most well-known verses in the Bible is this one: 'For God so loved the world that he gave his one and only Son, that whoever believes in him shall not perish but have eternal life' (John 3:16). This verse helps us to know that God loves and cares for us. We are loved. This sense of being loved is extremely important. God's love is supremely demonstrated in the action of Christ in coming to this world as a human being, to identify with us. Although He was in nature God Himself, and had created the world, He became man so that He could identify with our condition. Because He suffered pain and rejection, He can understand us when we go through great trials in our lives. Finally, on the cross we can see demonstrated the love of God for us. Christ there takes our sins on Himself and suffers and dies for us. This is love at its best and finest. Often in my life when things seem confusing and difficult, I turn to the cross and there see the reality that Christ loved me and gave Himself for me.

- The third area where the Christian faith impacts mental illness and helps someone to discover resilience is in the area of forgiveness. On the cross we see that when

Christ died, He offered forgiveness to those who crucified Him. Even in the agony of that death, He thought of others rather than Himself. He prayed to His heavenly Father, 'Father, forgive them, for they do not know what they are doing' (Luke 23:34). He continually thought of others, including His mother and His disciple John, even from the cross. Also, He was prepared to talk to a dying thief, who was crucified next to Him. When it became apparent that this man regretted and was repentant for his sins, Christ offered him a place in paradise. The Christian faith stands alone and apart from other religions in this understanding of forgiveness; somebody who has been living a reprobate lifestyle can turn back to the living God, and find total and utter forgiveness even at death's door. Other religions promise a possible paradise for good works, but in the Christian faith there is forgiveness available through the death of Christ.

- A fourth area of help for a person struggling with mental illness, given by the Christian faith, is that of meaning and direction. Many people live lives that consist of work, sleep, eating and television and the like, but without any real understanding of purpose in life. However, the Christian faith offers a very real reason to live. When an expert in the law gave his opinion regarding God's law, Jesus entirely agreed with him. This is the summary: '"Love the Lord your God with all your heart and with all your soul and with all your strength and with all your mind"; and, "Love your neighbour as yourself"' (Luke 10:27). If we obey these

214

commands, we are completing God's calling on our lives. We can, however, only act in God's strength, and many of us are very aware of our failings in these areas. We may not necessarily succeed all the time, but at least we know the direction we are facing. In this evil and troubled world, as we follow Christ we can learn to do good and love our neighbours as ourselves.

- The fifth area where the Christian faith has an impact on mental illness is in relation to finding support and help in our lives. Many people who have mental illness experience very little of this. In the Christian faith, the church can and should be a source of support and help. The church is a community where we are encouraged to love and care for one another. This can be vital when we go through tremendous struggles and difficulties. We are there for each other. I visit several churches of Sri Lankans in Cyprus and Israel and I find their needs are substantial. Even today as I am writing this, one girl has been unfairly dismissed from her employment and another is not being paid properly. However, I am impressed by the solidarity of the small Sri Lankan Christian community and their evident love for each other. This is expressed in very practical ways. This is the way things should be. Sometimes life issues are complex; however, we are here for one another, and I am encouraged that Sri Lankan brothers and sisters in Christ are able to help each other in the many difficulties and sometimes seemingly impossible situations which they face.

- The sixth area where the Christian faith has an impact on mental illness has to do with the power by which we live. In this book we have looked at a number of mental health conditions. We have become aware of the many factors that can come together in various combinations to bring about mental illness. We have looked at genetic factors, early life events and temperament and the like. We have considered the working of the brain and the actions of various neurotransmitters. We have looked at factors in our environment and how we can be affected by life events. The question has arisen as to what degree we can overcome the negative effects of certain situations or changes in our lives. In some conditions we cannot overcome the effects of the illness, particularly when there is evidence of marked organic change, such as in dementia. However, even here, we can ease suffering by showing care and compassion and ensuring that we treat people as people, rather than just dealing with their illnesses.

In some conditions, such as severe depression, we have observed that some people have endured the experience and come out of it stronger than before. We noticed this in some biblical characters and also in the lives of famous past Christian leaders such as Spurgeon and Judson. On the other hand, others faced with similar situations have felt crushed by the illness, or have become bitter and hard as a result. What lies behind the different ways people respond?

When we considered the fight in the brain in those facing certain addictions, we saw that some came through those battles and found answers and freedom from addiction, whereas others struggle on an ongoing basis. I retired from active clinical practice recently, and have since begun to visit a local hostel as a volunteer to talk to men who have a problem with alcohol addiction. There is a very positive atmosphere in the hostel, and the staff are very caring towards these men. However, as I talk to some of these men, I am keenly aware of the ongoing struggles they have in overcoming this addiction.

We have referred several times in this book to the excellent work of Professor Patricia Casey in her research article entitled 'The psychosocial benefits of religious practice'. We have thought about the issue of resilience and have considered how the Christian faith can strengthen this. How does this faith bring resilience in our individual lives? Let me give a brief illustration.

All of us will have been aware of the failure of an electrical gadget because of dead batteries. The source of energy needs to be replaced by changing the batteries. In a similar way, in our lives, we need to find a new energy source. In the Gospel of John we read as follows:

'Let anyone who is thirsty come to me and drink. Whoever believes in me, as Scripture has said, rivers of living water will flow from within them.' By this he meant the Spirit, whom those who believed in him were later to receive.
John 7:37–39

Jesus also gives this invitation to us:

'but whoever drinks the water I give them will never thirst. Indeed, the water I give them will become in them a spring of water welling up to eternal life.'
John 4:14

Jesus is telling us that a new source of power and divine energy is available to us. This is the power of the Holy Spirit. Jesus explains that the Holy Spirit will be like a river of running, or living, water within us.

I remember a few years ago standing behind the Niagara Falls and seeing and feeling the tremendous power of the waterfall just a few feet in front of me. In a similar way, there is no greater power than that of the Holy Spirit. When we open our lives to Jesus Christ, then He loves to come and indwell our lives in the person of the Holy Spirit. He comes in like a powerful flow of fresh water, to cleanse and renew our lives and to fill us with new energy and vigour. It is by the power of the Holy Spirit that men such as Judson and Spurgeon came through their trials. It is by this same power that we can endure our trials and come through them without bitterness or hardness. Jesus also promises that this water will be like a spring that brings eternal life. This eternal life is a new kind of life. It is the life of the Holy Spirit in us, and it continues into everlasting life. The Holy Spirit gives us power to live now and remains with us until we share life hereafter in God's living presence.

How can we receive this life? I suggest you look again at the end of chapter two of this book. There we talked about our life being like a car, and posed the question as to who was driving the car. We discussed whether we were in charge of our own life, or whether we had asked the Lord Jesus Christ to be in charge.

There is no better or more important decision than that of asking the Lord Jesus Christ to be in control of our lives. Here is a final prayer you could use to ask Him to take over your life.

Lord Jesus Christ, thank You that You became a man and showed through Your life Your love and compassion towards us. Thank You that You gave Your life on the cross to take away my sin. Thank You that You rose from the dead and that You hear me as I pray to You today.

Lord Jesus Christ, I ask You to be in charge of my life, and I turn away from all wrong and selfishness to give myself to You. I receive Your forgiveness. I ask for the Holy Spirit to come into my life to fill me today, in Jesus' name, Amen.

If you pray this prayer from the heart, God will bless you and come to you. Please let me know as well by emailing me: psychiatrist.sgc@gmail.com

May God bless you.

---

[1]Good Shepherd Schools India – RED International
www.redinternational.org/cafdw-gssindia (accessed 6th September 2015).

[2] Joseph D'Souza – Wikipedia, the free encyclopaedia: www.en.m.wikipedia.org (accessed 6th September 2015).

Further general resources

Professor Patricia Casey, http://www.ionainstitute.ie/ 'The Psycho-Social Benefits of Religious Practice': (accessed 4th September 2015).

Medication information: http://www.choiceandmedication.org (accessed 4th September 2015).

Christianity-Psychiatry http://www.mindandsoul.info/ (accessed 4th September 2015).

Mental health conditions information: www.patient.co.uk (accessed 4th September 2015).

Saneline mental health issues (helpline: 0300 304 7000); www.sane.org.uk (accessed 4th September 2015).

Young Minds – national charity to improve mental health of children and young people: http://www.youngminds.org.uk/ (accessed 4th September 2015).

NHS Direct (information Source on all health conditions): www.nhs.uk (accessed 4th September 2015).

Reading Well – Reading Agency (books on prescription on various mental health topics):

http://www.readingagency.org.uk (accessed 4th September 2015).

Raj Persaud, ed, *The Mind: A User's Guide* (A very helpful and easy to understand guide to mental health conditions.) (London, Bantam Press, 2007).

Harold G. Koenig *Faith and Mental Health: Religious resources for Healing*. (This is an extremely valuable resource and detailed analysis of the relationship between mental health and religious belief and practice.) (Templeton Foundation Press, 2005).

Mental Health Foundation, *Keeping the faith – Spirituality and recovery from mental health problems* (2007) (An interesting review which also describes several important faith-based initiatives in mental health care.) http://www.mentalhealth.org.uk (accessed 1st October 2015)

Mental Health Foundation *The impact of spirituality on mental health-A review of the literature* (2006) http://www.mentalhealth.org.uk (accessed 1st October 2015)

APSCC (Association for Pastoral and Spiritual Care and Counselling) *Resource Pack on Spiritual and Mental Health* http://www.mentalhealthmatters-cofe.org (accessed 5th October 2015).

Support groups: Details of numerous UK patient support organisations, self-help groups, health and disease information providers etc.

http://www.patient.co.uk/selfhelp.asp (accessed 4th September 2015).

Resources from the Royal College of Psychiatrists (many very useful leaflets are available): http://www.rcpsych.ac.uk/ (accessed 4th September 2015).

Cognitive Behaviour Therapy – free online interactive 'CBT: Living Life to the Full' http://www.llttf.com/ (accessed 21st August 2015).